RICHARD WAGNER'S MUSIC DRAMAS

Carl Dahlhaus

RICHARD WAGNER'S MUSIC DRAMAS

TRANSLATED BY MARY WHITTALL

CAMBRIDGE UNIVERSITY PRESS

CAMBRIDGE

LONDON · NEW YORK · MELBOURNE

Published by the Syndics of the Cambridge University Press
The Pitt Building, Trumpington Street, Cambridge CB2 1RP
Bentley House, 200 Euston Road, London NW1 2DB
32 East 57th Street, New York, NY 10022, USA
296 Beaconsfield Parade, Middle Park, Melbourne 3206, Australia

© 1971 by Friedrich Verlag, Velber
English translation © Cambridge University Press 1979

First published in German as *Richard Wagners Musikdramen*
by Friedrich Verlag in 1971
English translation first published 1979

Printed in Great Britain at the
University Press, Cambridge

Library of Congress Cataloguing in Publication Data

Dahlhaus, Carl, 1928–
Richard Wagner's music dramas.

1. Wagner, Richard, 1813–1883. Operas.
I. Title
ML410.W13D153   782.1'092'4   78-68359
ISBN 0 521 22397 0

CONTENTS

Introduction

The literature on Wagner is legion, yet it still owes its dominant features
to the non-musicians who were some of the earliest writers in the field:
Nietzsche, the composer's submissive and pedantic biographer Carl
Friedrich Glasenapp, and Hans von Wolzogen, who coined the term
'leitmotiv', to say nothing of Houston Stewart Chamberlain. For
decades writing on Wagner was compounded of wide-ranging, historico-
philosophical speculation, insatiable delight in the minutiae of his life,
however far-fetched or trivial, and a curious complacency when it came
to the study of the music, which hardly aspired to anything beyond
labelling the leitmotive. Views were stated in one of two tones of voice:
emphatic or enraged. And even today, a hundred years after the founding
of the theatre in Bayreuth, people who write about Wagner veer to one
pole or the other: to polemics or apologetics. (The writings of T. W.
Adorno in one corner and Curt von Westernhagen in the other are
sufficient illustration.) Yet at last, after the collapse of the false and
fateful apotheosis of Wagner under fascism, the belief seems to be
spreading that, while the artistic significance and standing of Wagner's
work are undiminished in the second half of the twentieth century, its
intellectual and political significance is now part of history and can be
regarded with the historian's detachment. We can look at Wagner
objectively without reducing our admiration for the music. While the
controversy over Wagner is far too tangled ever to be resolved – it can
only be dismantled and forgotten – it began to recede into the background
when hostility against Richard was diverted and redirected towards
Wieland Wagner and his productions of his grandfather's works.

It is no fluke that by far the greater part of Wagnerian literature is
biographical. Wagner was repeatedly seized by the compulsion to write

his own autobiography, either in outline or in the comprehensive format of the full-size book. Insofar as every book about him has been inspired not so much by the facts as by an earlier book about those facts, it is hardly surprising that historians and publicists alike have been challenged by Wagner's own autobiographical writing to continue, to supplement and to emend the account of his life, but above all to repeat it tirelessly. The story of Wagner's life has been told so often that it can be told no longer.

There is no reason why it should be. Nothing could be more mistaken than to take Wagner's works for musical autobiography. Concerned though he was about the authenticity of descriptions of his own life, Wagner himself, in his 1870 essay on Beethoven, deplored the common practice of tracing musical works back to biographical roots. He rejected the thesis that the Napoleonic associations of the *Eroica* had the least bearing on the symphony's music. The naive hermeneutics of the nineteenth century, for which music was an expression of a composer's emotions and experiences – the conviction, that is, that familiarity with the creator's life was essential to understanding of the works – found no support in Wagner's aesthetic theory. Indeed, Paul Bekker was not without justification when he tried, in his *Richard Wagner* (1924), to do exactly the opposite and illuminate the life from the work: musical drama, the plan that pressed for realization, summoned up the biographical events that were necessary to invest the outline, the emotional aura, the dim idea of a work with life and colour. *Tristan und Isolde*, Bekker argued, was not the outcome and expression of Wagner's love for Mathilde Wesendonk; rather, the love for Mathilde Wesendonk was a means whereby the dramatic conception took on musical and scenic shape. It must be admitted, in support of Bekker's thesis, that nothing mattered to Wagner but his work. He was as ruthless towards himself as towards others, and his life was merely the food on which his work fed.

In his earliest works Wagner was feeling his way, and there is nothing to distinguish them from those of any other composer hoping to establish a local reputation in the town where he earned his living as a kapellmeister. They illustrate the lack of stylistic direction, the uncertain eclecticism of the 1830s. *Die Feen*, after a tale by Gozzi, was a 'romantic opera' in the tradition of E. T. A. Hoffmann, Weber and Marschner. But at the time of its composition Romanticism was not so much a style rooted in the zeitgeist as one theatrical genre among others, an arbitrarily adopted posture. And it is characteristic rather than surprising that in his second opera *Das Liebesverbot*, based on *Measure for Measure*, Wagner elected to imitate Donizetti and Auber: the musical 'juste milieu', as Schumann called it. (Admittedly Wagner did not omit to explain and justify his change of style as if it involved a change of principle.)

It was only with *Rienzi*, a more ambitious conception than anything else he wrote before the *Ring*, that Wagner stepped out of the ranks of small-town kapellmeisters. A grand opera in the style of Meyerbeer and Halévy, *Rienzi* was intended for Paris: Wagner was convinced that the only way to reach every theatre in Germany, instead of remaining confined to one, was via Paris, the 'capital city of the nineteenth century'. (It was from Paris that Franz Lachner, the musical director of the Munich opera, got the libretto, at the very least, of his *Catharina Cornaro*.) The very fact that Wagner scorned to trouble himself about his local reputation in Riga, where he was employed while writing *Rienzi*, contributed to his ruin there: his response was flight, onwards to Paris. But the Grand Opéra refused to open its doors to him. It was not Paris but Dresden that *Rienzi* took by storm, and the ripples of that success did not spread far. Wagner's fame was eventually founded on *Tannhäuser* and *Lohengrin*, which were performed in very nearly every theatre in Germany during the 1850s (including the court theatres, in spite of the fact that by then Wagner was a political exile). Even so they brought him little financial gain, since only the most rudimentary form of musical copyright existed at that date: a consideration which ought to temper the righteous indignation of those who deplore Wagner's genius for spongeing.

The history of the growth of Wagner's fame has not yet been written, but it looks as though the decisive factor in the 1850s was the circumstance that the success of *Tannhäuser* and *Lohengrin*, slow to begin with but accelerating as it spread, coincided with the intellectual challenge thrown down by Wagner's theoretical writings, *The Artwork of the Future* and *Opera and Drama*. (The life of music is not so independent of writing about music as those musicians who despise theorizing like to think.) Not that there had been any shortage of treatises on operatic reform before Wagner; on the contrary, the lack of direction and the weaknesses of opera in Germany were a constant incentive to schemes for doing away with the dismal actuality and replacing it by something closer to each writer's ideal. What was new about Wagner was that his energy and ambition were not satisfied by mere theorizing about operatic reform, but were channelled into works that earned public approval and success. Nothing could be further from the truth than the idea that Wagner was 'misunderstood' (like Schubert or Bruckner). He encountered opposition enough, it is true, often of an ugly kind, but he never had to contend with the maleficent silence of neglect.

His position around 1860 was precarious, nonetheless. The earlier works, *Tannhäuser* and *Lohengrin*, were gradually losing their impact; the *Ring* remained a fragment – despairing of its completion, Wagner had abandoned it after composing the second act of *Siegfried*; the production of *Tannhäuser* in Paris ended in catastrophe, though so spectacular a one that Wagner's reputation was enhanced rather than the reverse; and *Tristan*, which he had intended to be a popular potboiler, had asserted its own will against its creator's and turned into an esoteric music drama. It was only with the success of *Die Meistersinger* in 1868, a success that won over even those who had hitherto resisted, followed by the foundation of Bayreuth in the 1870s, that Wagner became the uncrowned king of German music, a target of abuse perhaps, but possessing an importance that none could deny. There were other German composers of opera at the time: Heinrich Dorn (*Die Nibelungen*) and Carl Goldmark (*Die Königin von Saba*), Peter Cornelius (*Der Cid*) and Hermann Goetz (*Der Widerspenstigen Zähmung*); but that is a fact generally forgotten – not without reason. In the last thirty years of the nineteenth century the term 'German music' was synonymous with the music of Wagner. Even Paris, the city to which Wagner's thoughts always returned in assessing his own reputation, surrendered in the end.

Wagner rejected the expression 'music drama', which he interpreted as meaning 'drama for music'. It has nevertheless taken root, since his own expressions – 'artwork of the future', 'word-note-drama' (or 'drama of words-and-music'), 'action', 'festival drama' – are impracticable as titles for a genre. (Wagner was powerless to stop music drama, which was supposed to supersede opera, from becoming another recognized genre, just like opera.) But what is a music drama?

The challenging statement in *Opera and Drama* that in the 'artwork of the future' (the complement of, and the replacement for, opera, now in its decline) the drama was the 'purpose' or 'end' and the music 'a medium of expression' has often been badly misunderstood; it has been thought that 'drama' meant primarily the text, and that it was enough to analyse the relationship between words and music, the dependence of the music on the text, in order to understand the music as a 'medium' of the drama. But in musical drama the text is only one of the elements of the action, not its whole substance, and Wagner conceived of a greater overall goal, 'the unconditional, unmediated representation of perfected human nature'. Human nature, contorted and barely recognizable in modern, prosaic society, is to be restored by music, which, according to Wagner, has the power to recall archaic origins. The representation of human nature, however, of which music is a medium, is rather the province of the stage action than of the words.

If the concepts are distorted by the identification of 'drama' with 'text', things are further confused by the apparent discrepancies in Wagner's definitions, at different times, of the relationship between music and drama. The statement in *Opera and Drama* (1851) that music is a 'medium of expression' appears to be turned on its head nineteen years later in the essay on Beethoven (1870), which was inspired by Schopenhauer's metaphysics of music.

> Music, which does not represent the ideas inherent in the phenomena of the world

– let alone the phenomena themselves –

> but on the contrary is itself an idea of the world, and a comprehensive one at that,

– in other words, an element of metaphysics in sound –

> embraces drama as a matter of course, since drama in its turn expresses the only idea of the world sufficient to music.

Crudely paraphrased, it is not music that expresses drama, but drama music. And in 1872, in the essay *On the Term 'Music Drama'*, Wagner even refers to the dramas as 'deeds of music which have become visible'.

Obviously the aesthetic theory Wagner outlined in *Opera and Drama* was thrown into confusion, on the one hand by his reading of Schopenhauer, from 1854 onwards, and on the other by his experiences in the composition of the *Ring* and *Tristan*. The dogma lost its clear definition and the contradictions even affected the individual texts themselves. The Beethoven essay begins by hailing music as the source which 'includes drama as a matter of course', but a few pages later music is 'determined' by drama. The contradiction is mitigated, however, if we take into consideration that Wagner evidently employed the word 'music' in two senses: a metaphysical sense, for which he was indebted to Schopenhauer, and an everyday, empirical one. That metaphysically music is the source of drama by no means prevents it, as a 'manifestation of life' (as Wagner described it in his 1857 essay on Liszt's symphonic poems), from being 'determined' by drama; the drama is the 'formative motive' that the music needs for self-realization. The concept of 'absolute' music, founded in and sufficient unto itself, was a non-concept for Wagner: music is always determined from outside itself, by words, dance or stage action.

Der fliegende Holländer

1

The story of the Flying Dutchman, the subject of the work in which, according to Wagner, he abandoned his career as a 'manufacturer of librettos' and began that of a 'poet', has come down in a number of different versions. The one that influenced Wagner was Heinrich Heine's retelling of the legend in his *Memoiren des Herrn von Schnabelewopski* (1834), a version which Wagner praised as 'genuinely dramatic', and in which very nearly all the ingredients that he included in his libretto were already assembled.

I'm sure you already know the legend of the Flying Dutchman. It's the one about the doomed ship that can never make port and has been roaming the seas since time immemorial... That wooden spectre, that grisly ship owes its name to its captain, a Dutchman who once swore by all the devils in hell that he would sail round some cape or other – the name escapes me – in spite of the violent storm that was then raging, even if it meant sailing till Judgement Day. The devil took him at his word, and he must roam the seven seas until the day of judgement unless he is redeemed by the fidelity of a woman. Stupid as he is, the devil does not believe in women's fidelity, and so he allowed the doomed captain to come on land once every seven years and marry and try to work his salvation. Poor Dutchman! Time and again he was glad enough to be redeemed from marriage itself and to be rid of his redeemer, and then he went back on board ship.

The play I saw in the theatre in Amsterdam was based on that legend. Another seven years have passed; the poor

Dutchman, more weary than ever of his endless voyaging, comes on land, meets and makes friends with a Scottish merchant, sells him diamonds at a ridiculously low price and, when he hears his client has a beautiful daughter, asks for her hand in marriage. They agree on that deal too. Then the scene changes to the Scotsman's house, where the girl is waiting for her bridegroom with the greatest reluctance. Over and over again she looks sadly at a large, dilapidated painting hanging in the room, which depicts a handsome man in the costume of the Spanish Netherlands: it's a family heirloom and according to her grandmother it's a faithful likeness of the Flying Dutchman, as he was seen in Scotland a hundred years ago, in the time of King William of Orange. There is also a tradition attached to the painting, saying that the women of the family should beware of the original. For that very reason the features of this dangerous man have impressed themselves on the girl's heart since her childhood. So now, when the real live Flying Dutchman enters the room she is startled, but not afraid... She looks at him long and seriously and keeps looking sidelong at his portrait. It is as if she has guessed his secret and when he then asks her: 'Katharina, will you be true to me?' she answers resolutely: 'True unto death'.

Heine's narrator interrupts his description of the play here to tell the story of an adventure with a 'Dutch Messalina', who sometimes 'left her beautiful castle on the Zuider Zee and slipped off to Amsterdam incognito and went to the theatre, where she threw orange peel at any man who took her fancy, and sometimes even spent wild nights in seamen's taverns'. Heine did not tell the story of the Flying Dutchman for its own sake but for the sake of the ironic contrast; and detaching the two parts of the narrative from each other does him an aesthetic injustice.

When I went back into the theatre I was in time for the last scene of the play, where the Flying Dutchman's wife, Mrs Flying Dutchwoman, is standing on a tall cliff above the sea, wringing her hands in despair, while her unhappy husband can be seen out at sea, on the deck of his ghostly ship. He loves her, and is leaving her so as not to send her to perdition, and he tells her of his dreadful fate and the terrible curse that rests on him.

But she cries out in a loud voice: 'I have been true to you up to this moment, and I know a sure way of remaining true until death!' With those words, the faithful woman throws herself into the sea, and at once the curse on the Dutchman is lifted, he is redeemed and we see the phantom ship sink to the bottom of the sea.

The story of the phantom ship, condemned to sail the seas until Judgement Day, was already years, perhaps centuries, old when Heine used it in 1834. A short story on the theme was published in 1821. The new element in Heine's version, however, and the decisive one for Wagner, was the motive of the Dutchman being redeemed by a woman's fidelity. The fact that Wagner in effect repudiated the ironic gloss Heine chose to give the tragic tale is of no account. It was by no means uncommon in the eighteenth and nineteenth centuries, during the Sturm und Drang and Romantic eras, to ennoble old tales, which had sunk to the level of broadsheet ballads, by writing new, poetic versions of them. Tragic subjects were sometimes parodied, but parodies, vice versa, were also turned into tragedies.

It is not clear whether Heine, in the guise of Herr von Schnabele-wopski, was referring to a real or an invented Dutch play, that is, whether the motive of redemption, which became the core of the story for Wagner, was invented by Heine or taken by him from his source. Wagner himself did not know. In the first version of the *Autobiographical Sketch*, as it was published in 1843 in the *Zeitung für die elegante Welt*, he wrote:

> The genuinely dramatic treatment Heine invented for the redemption of this Ahasuerus of the ocean gave me everything I needed to use the legend as the subject of an opera. I came to an understanding about it with Heine himself.

But the later edition of the *Sketch* is less positive about Heine's authorship:

> It was especially Heine's treatment, taken from a Dutch play of the same title, of the redemption of this Ahasuerus of the ocean that gave me everything I needed to use the legend as the subject of an opera. I came to an understanding about it with Heine himself.

Wagner's biographer Ernest Newman was convinced that the 'understanding' with Heine was of a pecuniary nature, and that Heine claimed some kind of 'copyright', which Wagner later saw to be spurious. But no documentary evidence about their agreement has ever come to light, and it needs only the most superficial examination of Heine's text to lead to the conclusion that the Dutch play never existed.

The important thing is that, as Heine tells it, in spite of the interruption, the story is complete: the Dutchman's decision to leave Katharina, 'so as not to send her to perdition', follows on from her vow of fidelity without a break. The apparent sequence of intervening events, missed by Schnabelewopski, is a pretence. Consisting of nothing but an exposition and an abrupt catastrophe, the material is in fact more appropriate to a ballad than to dramatic treatment: the tale is complete in itself, but it would make a meagre play if presented as Heine tells it. This *quid pro quo*, whereby it is complete and yet incomplete, derives from the epic function of the legend of the Flying Dutchman, which is told in the *Memoiren des Herrn von Schnabelewopski* for the sole purpose of being interrupted by the story of the 'Dutch Messalina'. The aesthetic conditions Heine requires it to fulfil are complicated and contradictory: on the one hand – as the subject of a play – it must appear fragmentary, but on the other hand – as a story – it must be complete and provide an ironic contrast to the other anecdote, and it is only in conjunction that the two tales together form an epic whole. Once this has been understood, the artistic character of the narration and the skill with which it is deployed are so obvious that it is hard to believe in the existence of the Dutch play. The theatre visited by Herr von Schnabelewopski is an epic contrivance.

2

Another thing that would be quite unthinkable in a popular, tear-jerking play is the motivation, which is of a heart-breaking irony that can be attributed to nobody but Heine. In the narrator's words, the Dutchman leaves 'Mrs Flying Dutchwoman' 'so as not to send her to perdition'. But the perdition from which he wants to save her because he loves her is nothing other than her infidelity, which is inevitable unless she prevents it by precipitating her death.

Wagner, who rejected the parody, necessarily if he was to create a drama from the broadside ballad, provided a different motivation by elaborating the story. In place of the joking paradox, which is not merely the expressive form but also the stuff of Heine's version, Wagner needed an action able to fill out the third act of a drama. If infidelity is an inevitable destiny mocking the protagonists in *Die Memoiren des Herrn von Schnabelewopski*, in Wagner it is a tragic deception to which the Dutchman, made distrustful by his past experience, falls victim. The lay figure of Erik serves no other purpose than that of setting up the deception. Erik, whose love Senta accepts but does not reciprocate, tries to blackmail her with his own unhappiness, after she has made her vow to the Dutchman. By chance the Dutchman overhears Erik reproaching her and that is enough to arouse in him a suspicion as ill-founded and yet as understandable as Othello's.

Yet this misunderstanding, which appears to bring on the catastrophe, is not really a major dramatic motive but a device to conceal the kernel of the action, which is essentially undramatic, and to spin out the abrupt, wordless course of events to a stage action, fleshed out with words. Wagner had good reason to call *Der fliegende Holländer* a 'dramatic ballad': the tragic conflict that appears to be offered by the Erik subplot is an illusion.

From the very first there exists between Senta and the Dutchman an understanding that has no need of words, and is not accessible to language, at least not to rational dialogue. The central point of the work, the great duet in the second act, does not really break the silence in which the pair confront each other, but makes that silence resound; in precisely the degree that the tale of the Flying Dutchman does not make a drama it is, as Wagner instinctively recognized, predestined for opera. Far from causing a conflict that alienates Senta and the Dutchman, the misunderstanding resulting from Erik's intervention brings about what Senta has always longed for:

> Er sucht mich auf! Ich muß ihn sehn!
> Mit ihm muß ich zugrunde gehn!

> *'He seeks me! I must see him! With him I must perish!'*

The fidelity until death that Senta vows is a fidelity that is fulfilled in death: death does not merely place a seal of confirmation upon her fidelity, it is its inmost and even its sole constituent. The Dutchman needs Senta's fidelity, in order to be able to die; he denies himself the luxury of talking of love.

> Die düstre Glut, die hier ich fühle brennen,
> sollt' ich Unseliger sie Liebe nennen?

Ach nein! Die Sehnsucht ist es nach dem Heil:
würd' es durch solchen Engel mir zuteil!

'*The sombre flame I feel burning within me: am I, unhappy wretch,
to call it love? Oh no, it is the yearning for salvation: would that
it came to me through such an angel!*'

And Senta, who does not look for mundane married life with the
Dutchman, knows that the fidelity she vows is a votive offering. *Der
fliegende Holländer* does not belong in the traditional category of tragedy,
but in that of martyr plays, which lay down the paths along which the
protagonists, bent on self-sacrifice, can go to meet their ends.

On the other hand, it is hardly overstating the case to see an
anticipation of *Tristan* in *Der fliegende Holländer*. Senta and the
Dutchman create a world for themselves, just as do Tristan and Isolde,
in a hostile external world which has excluded the Dutchman, and from
which Senta withdraws voluntarily. And, like *Tristan* again, it is in the
contrast of night with the harsh, banal light of day that the action
assumes coherent allegorical form. The redemption the Dutchman seeks
does not consist in being allowed, through Senta, to re-enter the world
of day from which the curse has banished him; on the contrary, it is
Senta's decision to descend into his nocturnal world that brings about
his redemption.

The conclusion Wagner wrote for the overture in 1860, in the period
and in the style of the composition of *Tristan*, has a symbolic, revelatory
significance:

The motive on which the sequence is based comes from the end of
Senta's ballad, where it expresses the resolution to which the ballad has
driven her: 'Ich sei's, die dich durch ihre Treu' erlöse' ('Let me be the
woman who redeems you by her fidelity').

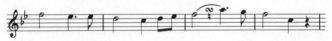

But the *Tristan*-like chromaticism, whereby the motive is modified and
altered, as it were, into recognition, expresses what was always latent in
Senta's desire to be the instrument of the Dutchman's redemption: the
yearning for death.

3

Although Wagner believed that with *Der fliegende Holländer* he had left the 'career of a manufacturer of librettos' behind him, the exterior form of the work, which he called a 'romantic opera', has more than one characteristic recalling the conventions that Wagner the theoretician despised, but which the practical man of the theatre found acceptable. The opening scenes of all three acts offer a good example. Each is divided into three in a similar way: a chorus which acts as a foil or background to the whole scene, an ensemble passage which reveals the situation, and an aria, whose espressivo is all the more effective for contrasting with the parlando of the ensemble. This was a grouping that settled into a pattern in nineteenth-century opera, and there is no denying that in the first two acts of *Der fliegende Holländer* Wagner, albeit unconsciously perhaps, was following the convention – one that was all the more powerful for its unobtrusiveness and apparent naturalness. As soon as the work of making an operatic libretto was undertaken, the subject was found to comply with the pattern as a matter of course, seemed even to call for it.

All the same, *Der fliegende Holländer* is no 'number opera' but a 'scene opera'. The process of drawing separate arias, duets, ensembles and choruses together in complexes, instead of having them succeed one another as separate items – a process adopted in act-finales in eighteenth- and early nineteenth-century operas – was extended in *Der fliegende Holländer* to the whole work, though without there being any question of calling it a through-composed music drama. We lack a recognized expression to define the technique and give it its aesthetic due: 'scene opera' is unfamiliar and may put people off. Wagner himself seems to have been fully aware of the terminological difficulty and tried to overcome it with agglomerate expressions like 'song, scene, ballad and chorus', but these serve to illustrate the problem rather than solve it. The lack of a term is not an irrelevance, insofar as in its absence the phenomenon for which it is needed is either imperfectly recognized or misunderstood altogether. The erroneous belief that operas are either number operas or through-composed music dramas is firmly rooted in the public mind. When that mind is made aware of the existence of 'scene opera', its reaction is to discount it as a transitional form, since it does not know how to classify it. But 'scene opera' is a form in its own right, and is the rule rather than the exception in the nineteenth century.

The combination of numbers in larger complexes can take various forms, ranging from simple succession to organic unity, but in every case it brings about a change in the form of the individual elements. Since they are no longer required to stand on their own they can be open in form; the recurrence of lines or stanzas, the construction of closed forms (whether song form A B A, or Bar-form A A B), can be dispensed with all the more readily, the more intimately the elements are linked together in a complex. The melodic writing is no longer bound by aria schemes but gains the freedom to match words and gestures at any moment in the dramatic situation. The development of expressive, declamatory arioso can be defined from the viewpoint of stylistic history as a compromise between recitative and aria, but so far as the evolution of compositional technique is concerned, the breakthrough was the replacement of the 'number' by the 'scene': as soon as formal cohesion was achieved by the grouping together in a scene of elements of different character, supporting and complementing each other, the individual parts themselves were relieved of the need to subject themselves to aria conventions and take closed forms, and the melodic writing was similarly liberated without seeming to be chopped up into heterogeneous fragments. The possibility of giving suitable dramatic form to detail was, paradoxically, a problem of large-scale form.

While the 'numbers' of *Der fliegende Holländer* are integrated into 'scenes' of so positive an overall character as to eliminate any danger of their falling apart in disconnected musico-dramatic instants, on the other hand there are two distinct actions, an 'internal' and an 'external', defined as well in dramatic as in musical terms. Just as the catastrophe, which brings the 'dramatic ballad' to its close, is doubly prepared – externally by the Erik subplot, internally by Senta's longing for death – so too the whole work is permeated by a similar duality of motivation. In the music this duality is so plain that the formal unity Wagner achieved by combining his 'numbers' in 'scenes' is endangered by a tendency towards stylistic heterogeneousness. Daland's bluff naivety, bordering on *buffo* (like Rocco in *Fidelio*), and the note of sentimental romance struck by Erik whenever he waxes lyrical are the musical handwriting of an 'exterior' action, distinguished from the 'interior' action – of which the Dutchman's monologue, Senta's ballad and their duet are the musical expression – by thundering triviality. It is hardly conceivable that Wagner set out to create the contrast by deliberately writing banal arias for Erik and Daland. But though they may not have been stale and conventional when they were written, around 1840, they have become so in the century and more since. And precisely because they have deteriorated into triviality they have become dramatically more effective, as the expression of the 'diurnal' world, than they originally were. It is because the aria in which Daland fussily commends the Dutchman and Senta to each other strikes us as intrusive – not just dramatically but musically as well – that it makes the silence in which they regard each other all the more eloquent.

Although it takes a rather different form here, the contrast between an interior and an exterior action still derives from operatic tradition: the distinction between recitative, which serves to further the plot, and aria, in which the action is suspended while lyrical reflection has time to spread itself. But in stylistic terms the contrast is turned on its head: it is the protagonists of the 'exterior' action, the movers of the plot in the conventional sense, who are inclined to fall into aria conventions, while the musical language of the 'interior' action, the language of Senta and the Dutchman, has developed out of the expressive declamation of accompanied recitative. What was the form of inward expression has been trivialized and so externalized, while the external form has been ennobled to serve inwardness.

4

As a ballad for the stage, differing from a drama in the modern sense by its tendency to abrupt alterations without rational motivation, *Der fliegende Holländer* is characterized – in precisely the central scenes of the 'inner' action – by elements that are closer to magic and fairy tales than anything else. Senta's second-act ballad, the kernel of the whole work, is not simply the story of the Flying Dutchman but a conjuration that brings him to the spot, in almost exactly the same way as Elsa's narration of her dream summons Lohengrin. In singing the ballad, too, Senta is herself made a part of it; she becomes, so to speak, a figure in the picture she paints. Finally, the moment at which the Dutchman appears in the doorway in answer to her summons similarly belongs in the twilight world of magic: it is as though the portrait of him, which has kindled Senta's yearning fantasies, has come to life. Remote regions and past times, the subject of fireside story-telling, are transformed at a stroke into the here and the now, and conversely the present time – or the piece of it in which Senta and the Dutchman have their being – seems to have been transported to the remote regions of fairy tale and to assume the colouring of the past.

The medium and the sole formal principle of modern drama since the Renaissance is dialogue: the form of verbal exposition and argument through which the protagonists define and discover themselves and the situation that governs and confines them. The goal of dramatic dialogue is a moment of decision when a character becomes aware of his moral autonomy and acts according to his inner motivation. But although Wagner conceived of *Der fliegende Holländer* as 'drama', as distinct from 'opera', it is precisely the central categories of drama that pale into irrelevance in it. The characters do not make or act on decisions, nor is dialogue the medium whereby they come to self-discovery. Decision based on moral autonomy is set aside by the working of a destiny that seizes on the characters from outside themselves and to which they submit unresisting, so that it completely fills their inner being. And dialogue is replaced, in the duet for Senta and the Dutchman at the heart of the work, by double monologue, which is in turn merely a cloak for silence.

> *Dutchman:*
> Wie aus der Ferne längst vergangner Zeiten
> spricht dieses Mädchens Bild zu mir:
> wie ich's geträumt seit bangen Ewigkeiten,
> vor meinen Augen seh' ich's hier...
>
> '*The sight of this girl seems to speak to me from the distance of long-lost ages; what I have dreamed for fearful eternities, I see here now before my eyes.*'
>
> *Senta:*
> Versank ich jetzt in wunderbares Träumen,
> was ich erblicke, ist es Wahn?
> Weilt' ich bisher in trügerischen Räumen,
> brach des Erwachens Tag heut an?
>
> '*Have I sunk into a wonderful dream? Is what I see an illusion? Have I dwelt until now in realms of deception? Is this the dawn of waking's day?*'

In terms of form, the consequence of the characters' passivity is that *Der fliegende Holländer*, as a ballad for the stage, should be called epic rather than dramatic.

The Dutchman's monologue in the first act differs acutely from monologues in classical drama in that it is not dialectical: it is not an interior dialogue, leading to a decision, but (particularly in the first section) a narrative that reveals something of the past. (The second and third sections, the prayer and the outburst of despair, though expressive, do not relate to that specific moment in the drama but amount to a kind of declaimed self-portrait, outlining the figure of the Dutchman independently of the place and moment in time.) Of course the monologue expresses the Dutchman's inner state, but in the manner of an omniscient narrator:

> Wie oft in Meeres tiefsten Schlund
> stürzt' ich voll Sehnsucht mich hinab:
> doch ach! den Tod, ich fand ihn nicht!

> '*How often have I plunged into the deepest pit of Ocean, longing for death – and have not found it!*'

While the Dutchman's monologue constitutes an epic element in the drama, Senta's ballad is a piece of exposition, though integrated into the course of the action to which it belongs. As a sung narrative it has the character of an interpolation: it is a song, sung in an opera whose language as a whole is singing. On the other hand, it is what sparks off Senta's resolution to be the sacrifice that the Dutchman yearns for. Yet it cannot be called a resolution in the sense of a decision arrived at by the processes of moral autonomy. What happens is that Senta suddenly perceives the destiny that has been laid down for her and which she blindly follows as though bewitched. It could almost be said that the ballad she has just sung takes possession of her.

There is another narrative we should mention here: at the moment when Erik is telling her about his dream, Senta, sunk in 'mesmerized sleep', is also dreaming it. The characters are subject to a power which comes upon them out of their inner beings and yet is alien to them. It is as though it is not Erik or Senta who speaks but – in Thomas Mann's words – 'the spirit of the narrative', which uses the characters merely as its mediums.

5

Ten years after composing *Der fliegende Holländer*, in *A Communication to my Friends*, the autobiographical essay of 1851, Wagner wrote about the development of leitmotivic technique, without actually using that expression, which was invented by Hans von

Wolzogen many years later. (His earliest, tentative experiments can be traced back as far as his first opera, *Die Feen*.)

> I remember that before I proceeded to write *Der fliegende Holländer* at all, I first sketched Senta's second-act ballad, composing both the text and the melody; in this piece I unwittingly planted the thematic seed of all the music in the opera: it was the poetically condensed image of the whole drama, as it was in my mind's eye; and when I had to find a title for the finished work I was strongly tempted to call it a 'dramatic ballad'. When I came eventually to the composition, the thematic image I had already conceived quite involuntarily spread out over the entire drama in a complete, unbroken web; all that was left for me to do was to allow the various thematic germs contained in the ballad to develop to the full, each in its own direction, and all the principal features of the text were arrayed before me in specific thematic shapes of their own making.

It is in fact a major exaggeration, or even a mistake, to speak of the 'thematic image' of Senta's ballad spreading out 'over the entire drama' – unless we are to interpret 'thematic image' and 'thematic germs' not so much as a specific, clearly outlined complex of musical motives but rather as a vague, though pervasive, poetico-musical mood, which is depicted in the course of the work in constantly altering melodic shapes, the inner relationship of which can be sensed, even though it is not necessarily discernible in the notes on the page. In all probability, when Wagner was writing the *Communication*, and looking back on his early works, the musical facts became intertwined in his mind with the idea of leitmotivic technique, with which he was preoccupied as he made ready to compose the *Ring*. (His writings almost always have something of the apologia about them; he was one of those revolutionaries who rebel in fear and trembling and almost against their own will, and therefore try to construct precedents for their innovations.)

There are only a few passages in the opera that are – if not governed or dominated – at least coloured by the basic motives assembled in the ballad, though they are admittedly key passages in the 'interior' action: the Dutchman's monologue, Erik's dream, some sections of the Dutchman's and Senta's duet and the finale of the whole work. The motivic technique, that is, is limited and rudimentary compared to that of the

Ring, and moreover the motives themselves, for all their prominence, are accessories, not really essential to the musical structure. Whereas in the *Ring* the motives both sustain and determine the musical development, those in *Der fliegende Holländer* have rather the character of motives of reminiscence and function as interpolations. The strictly regular recurrences of the Dutchman's motive in Erik's narration of his dream, for instance, mark the end of the lines of the text, but do not form the framework or backbone of the music. And the motives that symbolically introduce the duet for the Dutchman and Senta, those of redemption and of the Dutchman, stand out from the musical context like quotations or reminiscences, instead of constituting its substance. They have dramatic significance, but are not fully integrated in terms of the musical form.

The musical coherence of *Der fliegende Holländer* depends, not on a web of recurrent melodic motives, such as appeared to Wagner in retrospect as the decisively new characteristic of the work, but on the thoroughly conventional framework of the musical syntax. Even in the passages where the melodic writing is liberated from the aria tradition, such as Erik's narration of his dream and the duet for the Dutchman and Senta, it abides, almost pedantically, by the laws of established periodic structure, with bars in groups of $2 + 2$, $4 + 4$ and $8 + 8$. Later, when Wagner had rid himself of their sway, he ridiculed that kind of articulation as the 'squaring of compositional construction'. In fact, up to and including *Lohengrin*, Wagner departs more rarely from this 'quadratic construction' than does Beethoven, on whom he otherwise modelled himself. It would be mistaken, however, to assume that this use of regular periodic structures is the outcome of some technical weakness (attributable, perhaps, to Wagner's rudimentary education – which was not, after all, as rudimentary as all that). The schematic rhythmic articulation is rather the counterpart, the reverse face, of the emancipation of the melodic writing: in those stylistically more advanced passages of *Der fliegende Holländer*, where, in intention at least, 'opera' falls back and 'drama' advances, Wagner abandons the conventional means of founding musical coherence on the recurrence of melodic cells; the customary types of musical form, lending themselves to designation by alphabetical formulas such as A B A or A A B, disappear altogether or almost entirely. Each line of the text is sung to a unique, unrepeatable melody, which expresses the sense and intonation of the words or provides a musical equivalent of the movement that should accompany them. And it is in order to prevent the music from falling apart in disconnected fragments, as a consequence of the individuality of each line and phrase, that Wagner clings so obdurately and, on the face of it, inhibitedly to regular periodic structure. The schematicism of the syntax compensates for the melodic 'anarchy'.

Customarily the forms of melodies in opera and song alike are determined in two ways, by 'quadratic' syntax and by the regular recurrence of the same lines, creating effortlessly discernible, plastic shapes. Such familiarity tends to blind us to the recognition that these two formal elements do not necessarily have to go together, but can be alternatives; yet the recognition is essential if we are not to remain trapped in a superficial understanding of melody which favours hit tunes in opera – and even in music drama. If 'quadratic' structure is predominant in *Der fliegende Holländer*, notably in the semi-declamatory passages like the first section of the Dutchman's and Senta's duet, in the *Ring* regular syntax has been torn apart and dissolved in 'musical prose': phrases of unequal and irregular length succeed one another, without constituting the antecedent and consequent clauses of a period. But this syntactic irregularity in the *Ring*, reminiscent of *vers libre*, is compensated for by the constant recurrence of the same motives, the leitmotivic technique which embraces the whole drama, restoring through the melodic writing a musical coherence which has disappeared from the rhythm and syntax. In *Der fliegende Holländer*, on the other hand, motivic recurrence is, as I have said, a peripheral element; from the compositional viewpoint at least, it is not essential to the structure and does not need to be, because the musical form is guaranteed by the 'quadratic' syntax. However, this stability of melodic form, to which the work owes a not inconsiderable part of its popularity, exacted a price: the rhythmic regularity severely restricts the capacity of the musical phrases for individual, declamatory expressiveness – the element, that is, that for Wagner distinguished 'drama' from 'opera'.

Tannhäuser

1

The provision of an alternative title for a play, summarizing the argument or the gist of the plot, was fashionable in the eighteenth and nineteenth centuries. But Wagner's *Tannhäuser*, in full *Tannhäuser und der Sängerkrieg auf Wartburg* (Tannhäuser and the Singers' War at Wartburg) owes its double title to the work's origins, and betrays that, in writing his text, Wagner brought together material from two legends that had no connection with each other in the literary tradition.

> To the name of my hero Tannhäuser, I added the title of the legend that I had combined with his myth, although originally they had nothing to do with each other. To my regret, Simrock, whom I so greatly esteemed for his study and resuscitation of the old German legends, later took exception to this.

Wagner did not mention that the relationship between Tannhäuser and Elisabeth, the essential element in the work's dramatic coherence, was his own invention: as a poet in an unpoetic age, he preferred to play the role of a discoverer of buried treasure, not of an inventor; what was innovatory or modern lay open to the suspicion of being prosaic.

The version of the legend of Tannhäuser contained in *Des Knaben Wunderhorn* is in two parts. In a long introductory dialogue, Tannhäuser tears himself away from Dame Venus and her enchanted mountain, the Venusberg, a hell disguised as a paradise, where he has spent a year, possessed by the demons into which the gods of the ancient world had been transformed in the Christian Middle Ages. (They had not been forgotten, but were now understood to be infernal powers, not heavenly ones.) Tannhäuser's leavetaking from Venus is excessively rhetorical, in marked contrast to the bald, abrupt narration of the legend itself. The absolution that Tannhäuser begs of Pope Urban 'in sorrow and in penitence' is refused:

> The pope has a white staff, made from a dry branch: 'When this staff bears leaves, shall your sins be forgiven you.'

'In sorrow and suffering' Tannhäuser goes back to the Venusberg.

> But when upon the third day the staff began to burgeon, messengers were sent out, hunting high and low for Tannhäuser. But he was in the mountain again, and there he shall remain until Doomsday, when God shall be his judge.

This is the material of the beginning of the opera's first act and the conclusion of the third, and it is used there in forms suggested by the poem: the principal scene of the first act is in the form of dialogue between Tannhäuser and Venus, and the chief constituent of the last scene of the whole opera is the extended narrative of his pilgrimage to Rome. But the folk song was not Wagner's only source: he took what he needed from wherever he found it. (The efforts of the literary scholars among Wagnerians to make the oldest of the sources he studied the most important ones for his works testify more to their devotion to German antiquities than to their understanding of the processes of dramatic composition.) The fact that Heine's poem *Der Tannhäuser* is a parody did not prevent Wagner from adopting some of its features. Heine's Tannhäuser leaves Venus because he can no longer endure the cloying pleasures of her 'paradis artificiel'; his words 'Ich schmachte nach Bitternissen' ('I yearn for the taste of bitterness') correspond to the 'Aus Freuden sehn' ich mich nach Schmerzen' of Wagner's hero. And if, in his confession to the pope, the self-recrimination of Heine's Tannhäuser serves as a poor disguise for the praise of Venus, from whose bondage he cannot free himself, Wagner's Tannhäuser anticipates Amfortas in speaking of 'Sehnen, das kein Büßen noch gekühlt'.

The legend of the singers' contest, or 'war', at the castle of Wartburg belongs to a completely separate tradition, yet it does contain a few elements, not perhaps very prominent ones, which made the association with the Tannhäuser legend feasible. In the folk-song version of the latter in *Des Knaben Wunderhorn*, Venus's farewell words, half curse, half blessing, are: 'Wherever in the land you roam, my praise shall be your song.' In the opera it is precisely a song in praise of Venus that brings about the catastrophe during the singing contest. On the other hand, in the traditional story of the Singers' War, the astonishing and dismaying art of Heinrich von Ofterdingen, in the role Wagner assigns to Tannhäuser, is inspired by demons. E. T. A. Hoffmann retold this story in his *Die Serapionsbrüder*, and even introduced a mention of Venus and the Venusberg. The demon Nasias and Heinrich von Ofterdingen sing in turn a song in praise of 'the rapturous joys of the Venusberg': 'And it was as if the flames that flickered about Nasias were turned into fragrances breathing erotic desires and pleasures, perfumes in which the sweet notes rose and fell like tumbling cupids.' Hoffmann's words anticipate the phantasmagoria of Wagner's Venusberg.

It is this legend that provides the basis, in dramatic, visual terms, for the demonic confusion that Tannhäuser's song causes in the Hall of Song: a confusion in which shock and disgust are mingled with fascination. The complicated ghost story contrived by Hoffmann to invest Heinrich von Ofterdingen with magic powers was rendered superfluous by Wagner's idea of using the Tannhäuser legend as the background to the Wartburg legend. The combination of the two separate traditions gave shape to the drama that in Hoffmann's tale remained dormant.

On the other hand, it does appear at first as though the Wartburg legend has nothing to add to the Tannhäuser legend in function or significance. After the Venusberg has vanished as if by magic, as a result of Tannhäuser's cry of 'Mein Heil ruht in Maria', there is nothing to prevent him, if he feels the burden of his sins, from joining the pilgrims there and then, as they pass by him on the way to Rome. When he is unmasked as a sinner in the singing contest and sentenced by the Landgrave to make the pilgrimage as a penance, it is an external motivation which adds nothing to his inner motive, his longing for absolution, but provides an effective tableau for the second-act curtain.

What is really gained by linking the two legends only becomes clear if we recognize that the contest, filling the second act with theatrical parades and noisy disputes, is merely a façade, behind which the tragic relationship between Tannhäuser and Elisabeth works itself out almost wordlessly. We must hear his hymn in praise of Venus as Elisabeth hears it, pierced to the heart by his affirmation of the pleasures of the pagan goddess's hell. If today, well over a century after it was written, the song is tinged with triviality, a too easy vigour, it strengthens rather than diminishes the tragic, theatrical effect. Amid the noisy outrage of the knights as they turn on Tannhäuser with drawn swords, the soundless inner collapse of Elisabeth is the important event. She prevents the others from meting out rough justice to Tannhäuser, not because she is aloof to earthly tumult in her sainthood, but because the limited emotional capacities of the knights, even Wolfram, cannot rise to the level of what happens between her and Tannhäuser.

Tannhäuser is another Flying Dutchman, burdened by a curse from which he can be released only by a sacrificial death, that of Elisabeth:

> Nimm hin, o nimm mein Leben:
> nicht nenn' ich es mehr mein.

'Take, O take away my life: I call it mine no longer.'

The flowering of the pope's staff, the miracle of the Tannhäuser legend, is in Wagner's opera merely a visual metaphor for Tannhäuser's absolution through Elisabeth's death. Once he has been absolved he can die: in the first act, when Venus tried to prevent him from leaving, he countered:

> O Göttin, woll' es fassen,
> mich drängt es hin zum Tod.

'Goddess, try to understand that it is towards death that I am driven.'

But in *Tannhäuser*, unlike *Der fliegende Holländer*, death represents the end of an emotional delusion and confusion from which there was no escape route: Tannhäuser and Elisabeth die of their tragic predicament, without any manifest empirical cause. The Flying Dutchman is driven by a simple longing for death; Senta, as the heoine of her own drama of martyrdom, plays the part of the instrument of his redemption. But in *Tannhäuser* the threads of the drama of redemption become tangled. Tannhäuser's love for Elisabeth is a divided emotion, split from the first between passion, obsession and a persistent, covert recollection of Venus on the one hand, and a longing for redemption through the agency of the saint that Elizabeth is for him on the other; it is she whom subconsciously he already invokes when he escapes from Venus with the words 'Mein Heil ruht in Maria'. In Venus's 'paradis artificiel' he longs for starlight and the fresh green grass of springtime; but simple earthly pleasures are precisely what are denied him even in his love for Elisabeth, which, whether it is stamped by demonic possession or pious longing for salvation, is not truly human. The hymn of praise to Venus that strikes death into Elisabeth's heart expresses openly and publicly what already lay behind Tannhäuser's words to Elisabeth earlier in the second act:

> Den Gott der Liebe sollst du preisen,
> er hat die Saiten mir berührt,
> er sprach zu dir aus meinen Weisen,
> zu dir hat er mich hergeführt.

> *'It is the god of love whom you should praise, he plucked the strings of my harp, he spoke to you out of my songs, he led me to you.'*

The hymn to Venus reveals the true identity of the 'god' he means. When he confesses, in Rome, to a longing that no penance will assuage ('Sehnen, das kein Büßen noch gekühlt'), the memory of Venus still casts a shadow over that of Elisabeth. Wagner himself recognized that the ambiguity and confusion of the emotions gave the work its distinctive character, as we can see from a letter he wrote to Ernst Benedikt Kietz on 6 September 1842, at the time when *Tannhäuser* was still at the planning stage:

> I got them to show me Carlo Dolci's *Madonna* in the parish church in Aussig: I found the painting quite extraordinarily delightful, and if Tannhäuser had seen it I should have no difficulty in understanding how he came to transfer his devotion from Venus to the Virgin without any great access of piety. – Anyway, now I know exactly what the saintly Elisabeth should be like.

2

Tannhäuser's feelings and actions, like those of Siegfried in the *Ring*, are marked by impulsiveness and an extraordinary amnesia. He appears to be not completely in control of himself, a prisoner of the moment and of the emotion that happens to have hold of him. Events take place in abrupt oscillation between extremes. The 'art of transition' of which Wagner could later boast, pointing to the second-act duet in *Tristan* as the paradigm, is still undeveloped in *Tannhäuser*.

When Wolfram, 'with raised voice' as though pronouncing a conjuration, invokes the name of Elisabeth in the last scene of the first act, it appears to awaken in Tannhäuser, who is 'violently seized with joy', a memory that had been buried deep inside him. But his forgetting of the past is equally instantaneous and complete. When Elisabeth asks him where he has been during his long absence, Tannhäuser answers (it would be mistaken and imperceptive to interpret his words as an evasion):

> Fern von hier,
> in weiten, weiten Landen. Dichtes Vergessen
> hat zwischen heut' und gestern sich gesenkt.

'Far from here, in distant, distant lands. Dense oblivion has fallen between today and yesterday.'

Then in the third act, as he searches for the Venusberg, he seems to have forgotten Elisabeth completely, so that when Wolfram again speaks her name the recollection strikes him like an electric shock: 'He stands rooted to the spot, as if paralysed by a violent blow.' Memory turns into forgetting and forgetting into memory at a stroke, without transition.

This abruptness and lack of mediation between extremes are matched by a casualness about motivation in *Tannhäuser*, which is all the more noticeable in the light of Wagner's wellnigh pedantic insistence, in the *Ring*, on explaining causes and tracing reasons back to the very beginning of things. How Tannhäuser got into the Venusberg in the first place is as unclear and unexplained as the origins of his love for Elisabeth; it is hard to see a connection between these two elements of the prehistory, and it would be a waste of time to try. Essentially, Wagner's dramatic construction is governed by a law of form to which the content, the plot, has to accommodate itself: this law is the same for *Tannhäuser* as for *Der fliegende Holländer*, the *Ring* and *Tristan*. On the one hand, it always seems as though – regardless of the motivation or lack of it in the individual piece – each of the lovers has always had a subconscious picture of the other in his or her heart; on the other hand, the love that grips Senta and the Dutchman, Tannhäuser and Elisabeth, Siegfried and Brünnhilde, Tristan and Isolde, is violent and instantaneous: the prehistory, if there was one, is irrelevant. But the formal law that so governs the action of the drama originated in opera, even if Wagner adopted it in his music dramas, that is, his works from the *Ring* onwards.

Music in opera, broadly speaking, is affirmative and linked to the moment, the immediate present. It does not explain or connect but asserts and establishes; and it succeeds in giving the appearance of necessity to what is unmotivated, and credibility to what is absurd and inconsequential. The justification of abrupt contrasts and reversals of fortune through the wordless arguments of music, the exploitation of the musical phenomenon to compensate for the lack of dramatic coherence, are the very essence of opera. The 'art of transition' is alien to it. By contrast, in music drama, one of the essential ingredients of which is leitmotivic technique, threads are incessantly knotted together and connections established. Everything that happens recalls something earlier, to which it is linked by either causation or analogy. The whole work is held together by a dense network of motivation: musical motives are simultaneously dramatic ones and vice versa. Opera, its separate parts distinct from one another, so that one tidy segment of present time succeeds another, feeds on contrast, music drama on mediation. Opera emphasizes the plasticity of musico-dramatic form, music drama the logic.

3

The music of *Tannhäuser* was composed in Dresden in 1843–5, but in a sense it was never completed. Wagner made the first changes before he even left Dresden: whereas at the première the apparition of Venus and the death of Elisabeth in the third act were depicted only in the music, when the work was revived in 1847 the staging of the final scene was made more vivid by the appearance both of Venus and her train and of Elisabeth's funeral procession. For the Paris production in 1861 – a catastrophe in the short run but a triumph in the long – Wagner rewrote parts of the Venusberg scene and, less drastically, parts of the singers' contest. Then finally in 1883, a few weeks before his death, he told Cosima that he still owed the world *Tannhäuser*.

The compositional problem, as it seems to have presented itself to Wagner, was not one to be solved by mere revision. In the (second) Dresden version the music of the Venusberg scene is not exactly too weak in its motivic substance, but it is not sufficiently developed to provide an adequate counterpoise to the scenes dominated by the chorales, songs and marches, which are what stick in the memory and were the basis of the work's popularity: the musical character from which not even Tannhäuser's song in praise of Venus during the contest is free. (Even in the Paris version it is not so much this song, which Wagner decided not to meddle with, as a fleeting reminiscence of the Venusberg music in the orchestra which conveys Tannhäuser's alienation and inner distance from the other minstrels through the contrast in musical style.)

On the other hand the revision of 1860–1 resulted, in the Venusberg scene, in a sometimes abrupt juxtaposition of old and new sections, the stylistic discrepancy of which is only too obvious. The sound of the orchestra, thanks especially to the greater subtlety of the writing for woodwind, is of breath-taking refinement in the new passages. Nevertheless, the view that, although the musical superiority of the Paris version in some details is beyond dispute, its stylistic inconsistency makes it as a whole inferior to the Dresden version, is questionable insofar as it measures Wagner by a norm that is not necessarily appropriate. The demand for stylistic uniformity and consistency is classical at bottom, like the categories and tenets of conventional aesthetics as a whole; but Wagner, briefly, was a mannerist and a practical man of the theatre. The stylistic discrepancies may leave something to be desired aesthetically from the standpoint of abstract musical principles, but in a musico-dramatic light they can be seen to express the conflict between the everyday, natural world, to which Tannhäuser longs to return, and the artificial paradise where Venus seeks to keep him: it is no accident that it was the part of Venus, not of Tannhäuser, that was rewritten. Of course Wagner the aesthetic theorist was acquainted with classical postulates such as stylistic unity, and so he was naturally concerned by the discrepancies of the Paris version.

The technical and aesthetic contradictions (technical elements are always aesthetic as well, just as aesthetic opinions always need a technical basis) are well illustrated in Venus's aria 'Geliebter! Komm'. Calling it an 'aria' may cause surprise and be regarded as sacrilege against the Bayreuth dogma which recognizes the existence only of 'scenes'; it has not been chosen as an easy way out of a terminological embarrassment, however, but has the justification that the passage in question – contrary to what might be expected – displays stricter formal unity in the Paris version, dating from the era of the music dramas, than in the Dresden version, which goes back to the period of the operas. The aria, over 100 bars in an expansive tempo (andante), can be divided, broadly speaking, into two parts, 'Geliebter! Komm' and 'Aus holder Ferne'. The first was there in outline in the Dresden version and was adapted for the Paris version, with new music for the orchestra, transposed from F$\sharp$ to F, and in 3/4 instead of the original 4/4; the second part was new. It is typical of the Paris version that the beginning of the first part is identical to the conclusion of the second (*a* represents an introductory motive, *b* the principal vocal motive):

I   II
a^1 b^1 b^2...b^3...a^2...b^4 b^5 a^3

(a)

(b)

Thus the Paris version is rounded off with a reprise, which is not the case in the Dresden version, in which Wagner through-composed the text without recalling earlier material. (A recurrent orchestral motive, which played a structural role there, is reduced to a brief allusion in the introduction in the Paris version.)

The reprise, which remotely suggests the pattern of a *da capo* aria, is not the only element linking the two parts together. It is the additions to the first part which betray Wagner's leaning towards formal integration: there is the recurrence of the principal motive at the end of the first part (b^3), and there is the introductory motive (a^1), which is used again at the beginning of the second part (a^2) and again, this time in the voice, at the end (a^3).

An analyst who took as his starting point the aesthetic dogmas that – implicitly rather than explicitly – provide the basis of traditional musical formal theory might be inclined to regard the formal unity of Venus's aria as the consequence of the 'quadratic' rhythmic construction, the articulation according to regular four-bar groups, which in turn is due to the structure of the verse. That would mean that Wagner was more conscious of the aesthetic connection between rhythmic and formal regularity or schematicism in 1860 than in the 1840s. Illuminating though it may appear, this is in fact the wrong explanation. In Wagner, the creation of formal coherence by the repetition of motives and melodic phrases, as has already been seen in the chapter on *Der fliegende Holländer*, appears rather in compensation for rhythmic irregularity than as the consequence and analogy of regularity.

The through-composed Dresden version of the aria is constructed almost entirely in four-bar groups; the sole exception is a three-bar group ('ein Freudenfest') which is, however, simply a contraction of a melodically analogous four-bar group ('der Liebe Feier'), that is, it modifies the regular pattern but does not depart from it. On the other

hand, even though it runs counter to the structure of the verse, there
is an unmistakable tendency in the Paris version towards irregular
rhythms or 'musical prose'.

The bars composed for the Paris version at the end of the first part
of the aria ('Komm, süßer Freund') are still based on a 'quadratic'
formula, a sequence of 2 + 2 bars, but it is almost imperceptible, so
overlaid is it by the accompanying elaboration of the opening idea and
the extra final bar. The irregular, flexible rhythm is balanced, however,
by the regular, closed form.

It is perfectly possible to categorize the phantasmagorical effect, the
musical magic, of the Paris components of the Venusberg scene in
technical musical terms, in spite of the suspicion with which Wagner
himself regarded technical analysis, preferring to pass off the artificial
under the appearance of naturalness. To name one factor at least, the
magical effect owes something to the way that the melody and the
harmony are brought so close to each other that the customary
distinction, fundamental to the listener's power of perception, between
melodic foreground and harmonic background, between figure and foil
in the language of Gestalt psychology, falls into abeyance. The listener
has the sensation of losing his normal footing and of being in a state of
musical suspension.

In the bars introducing Venus's aria, which depict musically the spell she
attempts to cast on Tannhäuser, the same notes are heard as melody in
the principal parts (the solo violin and the violas) and as chordal

accompaniment in the subsidiary parts (the rest of the violin section divided). It would be a waste of time and effort to seek to define whether the four-part writing for the accompaniment should be regarded as drawing the notes of the melody together in chords, or whether the melody notes in the principal parts were selected from the four-part harmony writing. It is precisely the lack of differentiation between the elements that creates the aesthetic effect.

4

Tannhäuser is an opera, not a music drama. Though Bayreuth dogma has it that Wagner's earlier works, too, are consistent in their use of leitmotivic technique, the principle does not apply, strictly speaking, to any work before the *Ring*. The technique is still rudimentary in *Tannhäuser*.

Wagner's musical language in this work is at a stage of its development where the systematic use of leitmotivic technique is not yet possible. This is demonstrated by the fact that it is sometimes hard to distinguish with reasonable certainty between a musical analogy, cloaking an allegorical intention, and chance melodic resemblance.

Although the association between the motives quoted here is undeniable when they are placed side by side like this, it is extremely difficult to assess the significance of it – unless one settles for an omnivorous symbolism that draws metaphysical satisfaction from linking everything with everything else.

There is nothing 'leitmotivic' about the recurrence of Tannhäuser's song in praise of Venus in the singing contest, or of the chorales of the older pilgrims, unless we choose so to regard the fact that the two chorales, which otherwise bear no resemblance to each other, have a pair of lines in common, which stand out of the deliberately archaizing 'old

German' context by reason of their un-chorale-like chromaticism, and are a musical gesture of suffering, alluding to Tannhäuser. But as a whole these choruses are virtually incidental music, not completely integrated into the musical fabric; even the motive expressing the curse hanging over Tannhäuser has the character of a musical stage property.

The only motives that function as leitmotive when they recur are those from the Venusberg scene. But for all their associative significance and recognizability, they are not wholly individualized and that is what distinguishes them from the motives in the *Ring*. It hardly matters which of the five or six motives is quoted to recall the Venusberg scene: in the singing contest, the Paris version occasionally brings in other motives than the Dresden version. None of them does more than allude to the realm from which they come, and they do not possess distinct, allegorical meanings peculiar to any one of them singly. Insofar as it is possible to speak of leitmotivic technique in *Tannhäuser* at all, it is still being manipulated *en bloc*.

There are anticipations in *Tannhäuser* of the compositional elements which, ten years later, formed the associations in the fully developed leitmotivic technique of the *Ring*, which only then added up to Wagner's 'system', as some contemporaries called it. But in the earlier work these prototypes are random and have no bearing on each other; it would be mistaken to give them in their isolation a significance that they were to derive only from the fact of their coming together.

If the quotations from the Venusberg music that interrupt the singing contest, as if rising out of the unconscious mind, perform one leitmotivic function in that they recall something from the past and provide psychological or allegorical links between different parts of the drama, on the other hand they differ from motives in the *Ring* by the way in which they seem to be inserted into the musical text from without, instead of constituting its framework or fabric. They have the character of interpolations, of additions; it is significant that, in the Paris version of Venus's aria, Wagner was able to cut the references to the Bacchanale that bracket the segments of the aria together in the Dresden version, without weakening the melodic structure. With the periodic construction of the melody, the motives of recollection became no more than musical parentheses and could safely be abandoned.

Things are different in Tannhäuser's narration of his pilgrimage to Rome, musically and dramatically the heart of the third act; here the motives, given primarily to the orchestra, form the framework of the musical structure: they are not now accessories but essential elements. But unlike the motives from the Venusberg scene they do not have the significance of leitmotive: their use is confined to the narration itself, instead of being developed as a motivic web spread out over the whole drama. (Of course, the orchestral prelude to the third act, the counterpoise in abstract musical form to the vocal monologue, contains reminiscences of earlier material and anticipations of motives from the narration, but that has more to do with overture tradition than with leitmotivic technique.)

The decisive factor was the development of the musical structure ('die Tonsatzkonstruktion', as Wagner called it). Had that not undergone the profound transformation that it did, leitmotivic technique, the idea of extending the system of leitmotive throughout an entire work, would have remained an abstract concept without a footing in musical reality: the idea of a poet rather than of a composer.

The Rome narration is a paradigm of the transitional stage in the development of the compositional technique, midway between 'no longer' and 'not yet'. In it is defined the problem which is to be solved by the musical phrase structure, the correlative of leitmotivic technique and the foundation on which it was to be erected.

The first motive in the narration, characterizing its first section ('Inbrunst im Herzen'), hesitates somewhere between an orchestral figure supporting the vocal line, as it might be a figure in the accompaniment of a song, and a leitmotiv in the *Ring* sense.

The motive is undeniably eloquent and clearly shaped: a musical gesture of unmistakable expressive content. But it is not so well formed and vivid that it cannot bear the fivefold repetition it receives, without interruption by other motives; it is hard to imagine any of the more prominent leitmotive in the *Ring* lending themselves to this kind of ostinato repetition. To the extent that the motive has the character of an unassertive accompanimental figure, it allows the vocal melody all the breathing space it needs to achieve a happy medium between declamation and arioso. This orchestral motive's lack of vividness and independence is of positive benefit to the melodic flow.

By contrast the principal motive of the second section ('Nach Rom gelangt' ich so'), which anticipates one of the melodic types of *Parsifal*, is so pregnant and self-sufficient that the vocal line is confined, to all intents, to mere repetition of its notes.

It could be said to provide the foil for the orchestral motive.

Thus either the vocal melody subordinates the orchestral motive, or vice versa. The relationship between voice and orchestra is as yet precarious and not well balanced. Yet there is discernible, mediating between the compositional extremes found side by side in the Rome narration, the germ of a method of composition that promises to create a rapprochement between the arioso-declamatory style of vocal melody and the expressive and allegorical motivic writing for orchestra: a goal towards which Wagner was still feeling his way in *Tannhäuser*.

Lohengrin

1

Lohengrin, dubbed a 'romantic opera' by Wagner, is something of a paradox: it has a fairy-tale subject, a tragic outcome and the outward trappings of a historical drama. Mutually exclusive opposites, myth and history, fairy tale and tragedy, are forced together without any of them suffering perceptible harm. *Lohengrin* is the apogee of the genre of romantic opera and proves its claim to universal poetic worth.

At the heart of the Lohengrin legend is the story of the Swan Knight, one of those fairy-tale themes symbolizing the ineradicable dream of rescue from adversity by some miracle. In his *Deutsche Mythologie*, which Wagner read, Jacob Grimm wrote: 'The medieval literature of the Lower Rhineland and Low Countries is full of similar legends of the sleeping youth in a boat, drawn by a swan to a land in need of succour.' And Lohengrin's loss of his magic power at the moment when he is forced to reveal his name is another fairy-tale motive with origins in sorcery.

In his epic poem *Parzival*, Wolfram von Eschenbach gave the myth a semi-historical setting. Loherangrin, Parzival's son and a knight of the Grail, is sent by the Grail to Antwerp, to defend the Duchess of Brabant against the princes of the province, who are forcing marriage on her. A Christian reason is given for forbidding the duchess to ask his name, but the prohibition cannot shake off its fairy-tale origins.

> 'Lady, I shall lose much if I am to be ruler in this country. Hear my request: never ask me who I am. It is on that condition alone that I may remain with you. If you ask, then you will lose me in spite of your love. God has warned me of the consequences if you do not heed my warning. He knows the reason why.' She gave her woman's word – which love later made her break – to obey his command and always to do as he asked.

Here Wolfram suggests the tragic dilemma which dominates the action of Wagner's drama: it is Elsa's love which drives her to disobey the command on which the fulfilment of her love depends. It is the means whereby her love is expressed that leads to its destruction.

The tale is briefly told by Wolfram, but he was also wrongfully credited with the authorship of an anonymous *Lohengrin* of the later thirteenth century (a howler for which the only possible excuse is the unsatisfactoriness of 'Anon.' as an attribution). This version inflated the story by the addition of thousands of lines (mainly martial in content), and Wagner took from it only the dating of the action in the time of King Henry the Fowler (r. 919–36) and his wars against the Hungarians, and the plot-motive of Lohengrin's defeat of Count Friedrich of Telramund, an aspirant to Elsa's hand and the throne of Brabant, in a duel which exposes Telramund's claims as fabrications.

Wagner improved on the anonymous epic, which he found 'meagre' and 'insipid', by adding elements of magic and fairy tale, thereby reversing the process of historicization it had undergone in the thirteenth century. He introduced the heathen black magic of Ortrud, Telramund's wife, to oppose Lohengrin's white magic. When he wrote in a letter of 4 August 1845, 'my own powers of invention and creation play the greatest part in this work', he was referring above all to the figure of Ortrud, the most active force in the outward action, in which she provides the visible counterpart to Lohengrin that Wagner's theatrical instinct knew was necessary. Ortrud turns Elsa's young brother Gottfried into a swan – the very swan that brings Lohengrin from the Grail castle Monsalvat to Antwerp – and it is she who incites Telramund to accuse Elsa of Gottfried's murder. (In Wagner Telramund is as much deceived as deceiver.) Finally, it is Ortrud, following Telramund's defeat by Lohengrin, who wakens fear and doubt in Elsa's mind, so that the inner compulsion to ask him the question he has forbidden her becomes overwhelming. It is, incidentally, typical of Wagner that he stylized this dramatic antagonism as a conflict of world history, the confrontation of paganism and Christianity: to be musically productive he needed wide horizons.

The fact that in some scenes *Lohengrin* is decked out with all the panoply of historical drama, with processions and tableaux smacking of *Rienzi* and grand opera, should not be misinterpreted as regression to an earlier stage of Wagner's development, ignoring the advances he had made in *Tannhäuser*. Classifying the work by crude stylistic traits, tidily assigning it to a musico-historical pigeon-hole, misses the point that everything has a dramatic foundation. The conflict Lohengrin – an Undine in knightly guise – has to face, the confrontation between the transcendental world he comes from and the earthly world he longs for, would remain pallid and incomprehensible if the mundane, temporal reality were not vividly characterized by historical colour and solid locations. The setting of an unhistorical, fairy-tale world would nullify the conflict that destroys Lohengrin. Unlike the *Ring*, in which the real and unreal worlds overlap as easily as if they belong to the same sphere, in *Lohengrin* the two worlds are clearly separated. The contrast is not to be played down, if Lohengrin's tragedy, which is founded in the irreconcilability of the differences, is to be brought home on the stage. 'Stylistic' unity would be a dramatic failing.

The historical elements in *Lohengrin* are there to provide a contrasting foil, not because Wagner still retained any affection for historical drama for its own sake. His painting of the historical details, culled with almost pedantic care from Jacob Grimm's *Deutsche Rechtsaltertümer* (Antiquities of German Law), is comparable to the technique of orchestral writing that he was developing simultaneously, the provision of melodically independent phrases for the subordinate parts, giving them the opportunity for individual expression. They are not heard as separate, distinct parts, but the fact that they have something to say, even though we do not understand it in detail, contributes to the richness and differentiation of the whole. Wagner the musical fresco painter was also a miniaturist – to the greater good of the mural effect.

But even if *Lohengrin*'s historical setting is only one facet of the work, it has an aesthetic significance as well as a dramatic one. In the context of operatic history it justifies the tragic ending, which was still unusual in opera in the mid-nineteenth century. It was accepted only in the grand operas of Meyerbeer and Halévy with their historical subjects. That Wagner did not relinquish the conventional link between tragedy and historical subject matter in *Lohengrin* shows he still relied in some respects on the operatic tradition against which he inveighed.

The fact that a happy ending was the norm in the opera of the eighteenth and early nineteenth centuries, which took its material primarily from classical myth and later from fairy tale, should not be dismissed as mere convention; there is good reason for it in the nature of the medium. With music the dominant element, laying down the genre's laws, opera naturally inclines towards (to use an eighteenth-century expression) the 'marvellous': to myth or fairy tale. Conversely, in a work with a 'marvellous' subject, it is appropriate that music, with its power to make the supernatural credible, should predominate. But the effect of music is conciliatory: however much the horrors pile up, we will not be shaken in our faith that where there is singing things cannot be as bad as they seem. The fact that Gluck's Furies sing, as well as Orpheus, gives us hope; we are confident that a rage that expresses itself in song will allow itself to be appeased. The happy ending of *Orfeo* has been criticized as a concession to audiences who were unable to stomach the severity of classical tragedy, but those same audiences demonstrated a capacity for taking the tragic subjects of plays in their stride, however harsh the fate of the protagonists; their preference for happy endings in opera simply means that the music raised their expectations of a conciliatory outcome to the tangles of the drama.

On the other hand, when the subject of the opera is historical, its relative realism imposes limits on the music's hegemony – at least in aesthetic expectations – and allowance has to be made for the possibility of a tragic ending. Wagner himself, in fact, was not fully convinced of the aesthetic legitimacy of the ending of *Lohengrin*. On two occasions he allowed himself to be persuaded, momentarily at least, by Hermann Franck in Dresden and some years later by Adolph Stahr, that he ought to alter the ending. His doubts are pardonable, not from the dramatic point of view, but as regards the aesthetic conventions of the genre. For *Lohengrin* occupies an area midway between historical drama and fairy-tale opera: this duality is not an aesthetic failing, however, but the stylistic exterior of the work's dramatic kernel.

2

As a romantic opera *Lohengrin* is the perfect realization of the pattern that Weber created for *Euryanthe*: like a prototype, the earlier work is subsumed in the later. *Euryanthe* has long been numbered with those operas that are famous but forgotten, a fate it owed not only to its unspeakably silly libretto but also to the misfortune of having been ousted from the repertory – even the ideal repertory that finds room for unique works – by *Lohengrin*, much as Rossini's *Otello* was replaced by Verdi's. (Sometimes it is hard, wellnigh impossible, not to break the aesthetic law that different works cannot be compared.)

Weber's Adolar, who is as stupid as only a hero can be and weak to boot, stands no comparison with Lohengrin, but Euryanthe's likeness to Elsa is undeniable, while the pair who plot their downfall, Lysiart and Eglantine, could pass as the models for Telramund and Ortrud. The similarities only serve to throw the crucial differences into relief, however. Telramund, the deceiver who is himself deceived, is a far more intelligible dramatic figure than the cynic Lysiart whose perfidy, while unexplained, offers no mysteries; and Ortrud, representing the pagan alternative to the world of the Grail, rises immeasurably high above the trivial jealousy of Eglantine. Romanticism is mere window-dressing in the text – though not the music – of *Euryanthe*; the plot is a stock dramatic subject, capable of existing behind any number of stylistic façades; and the inevitable happy ending is never in any doubt, even when the misunderstanding is at its worst. By contrast, it is the catastrophe that is alone certain in *Lohengrin*, the reasons for it rooted in the very heart of the work. The plotting that appears to bring it about is in fact nothing but a reflection cast on the surface by the inner action in order to be more acceptable on the stage, or indeed to take dramatic form at all.

The condition Lohengrin lays down is impossible of fulfilment; Elsa would have to ask him his name, even without Ortrud's interference – even if, as in Wolfram, only after the passage of years. By comparison with *Tannhäuser*, as Paul Bekker wrote,

> it was precisely in the inevitability of the conflict that the decisive element lay. That inevitability, which is understood as tragedy in the theatre, was the primary element in the overall design, the new creative idea.

The dullest-witted member of the audience must realize that there is no escaping the catastrophe by, at the latest, the end of the second act, the scene on the cathedral steps. Elsa still suppresses her doubt, as she calls the compulsion to ask the forbidden question, but she no longer denies its existence:

Hoch über alles Zweifels Macht
soll meine Liebe stehn!

'My love shall prove beyond the reach of all power of doubt.'

The beginning of the third act, the scene in the bridal chamber, serves only to postpone the inevitable. The derision the scene has always provoked stems from the kind of perception that isolates things that should be related to the dramatic context, and fails to see the ambiguous twilight in which the scene is shrouded. The bridal chorus itself, which ought never to be torn from its context, sounds different when the listener hears it against the shadow cast over the scene by the hopelessness of the situation. The innocuousness of the music, which has helped the piece to a misconceived popularity, is oppressive when it is heard in context.

In 1851, in *A Communication to my Friends*, Wagner wrote:

> Lohengrin sought a woman who would believe in him: who would not ask who he was or whence he came, but would love him as he was and because he was what he appeared to her to be. He sought a woman to whom he would not have to explain or justify himself, but who would love him unconditionally. For this reason he had to conceal his higher nature, for it was precisely the non-discovery, the non-revelation of this higher nature (higher because, to speak more accurately, it has been raised up) that was his sole guarantee that he was not admired or marvelled at or humbly – and uncomprehendingly – adored simply because of that quality. Admiration and adoration were what he did not seek; only one thing could release him from his isolation and satisfy his yearning: love, to be loved, to be understood through love. All his highest thinking, his most conscious knowing, were filled with no other desire than to be a complete, whole human being, swayed by and received with the warmth of human emotion, to be human entirely, not a god, i.e. an absolute artist. So he yearned for woman – the human heart. And so he descended from his blissful, barren solitude when he heard a cry for help rising from the midst of humanity from this particular heart, from this woman. But he is unable to shake off the telltale aura of his higher nature; he cannot help but appear an object of wonder; the amazement of the commonalty, the venom of envy throw their shadow even into the heart of the loving woman; doubt and jealousy prove to him that he is not understood but only adored, and tear from him the confession of his divinity, with which he returns into his solitude, destroyed.

Lohengrin is the tragedy of the absolute artist.

But Wagner's comment, which is coloured by the mood of his years in exile, obscures rather than illuminates the tragic antithesis at the heart of the work. In essence, the goal for which Lohengrin yearns is barred by the means whereby he seeks to reach it. The condition he makes (forbidding Elsa to ask his name), so that he can be sure she loves, not worships, him, might be possible for someone to keep who worshipped him and remained shyly at a distance, but it is impossible for someone who loves him as a human being. In seeking to annul what sets him apart from others, Lohengrin only succeeds in reinforcing it.

Wagner was surprised and disappointed, as he said in the *Communication*, that some commentators, and those not the most negligible, found the figure of Lohengrin, in whose tragedy he saw a reflection of his own, 'cold and obnoxious'. This was obviously a misconception on their part, yet is is not altogether unpardonable. Since Lohengrin can never deny his origins, although he feels, or yearns to feel, as a human being, it is easy enough to misinterpret his love for Elsa as a favour that he graciously bestows on her. It is not apparent that his love for her is vulnerable and dependent; or it becomes apparent too late, in his lament in the third act. At no time does he ever show a trace of fear. He closely resembles Wagner's Wotan, a god with human feelings, but where Wotan's divinity, in spite of the underpinning it receives from the Valhalla motive, loses credibility in the pitiable situations he lands in, in Lohengrin's case the difficulty is to recognize the humanity behind the supernatural emanation, to which the stage action and the music, above all the reactions of the chorus, repeatedly draw attention.

This dramaturgical difficulty extends its shadow over the music too. The musical climax of the third act is not Lohengrin's lament ('O Elsa! Was hast du mir angetan?') – a melodically rather uncharacteristic piece of operatic music with a sometimes disagreeable *Schwung* – but his Grail narrative ('In fernem Land'), which, as a reprise of the prelude to the entire work, marks the conclusion of the inner action that has been shaped by the music. Drawn down into an earthly environment by Elsa's narration of her dream, Lohengrin is carried off from it again by his own narration about the Grail kingdom. The presentation in epico-musical form is the realization of what it depicts: the narrations, during which the action apparently stands still, in fact contain its determining elements. The significance of that is nothing less than that the music of this 'romantic opera', the only thing that makes Lohengrin's appearance as the realization of Elsa's dream credible, is endowed with a fundamental motivating function.

3

Richard Strauss, whose worst enemies would not accuse him of lacking a sense of what works in the theatre, praised one scene in *Lohengrin* that a superficial listener, armed with preconceived ideas about 'operatic drama', might single out as holding up the action downright undramatically. This is the ensemble 'In wildem Brüten muß ich sie gewahren' at the end of the second act, marking the moment when doubt gains the upper hand in Elsa and the inevitability of the catastrophe becomes an overwhelming conviction, although Elsa is still just able to suppress the question. Nothing happens; it is a musical expression of expectant stillness, what the various characters sing is only a substratum of the music, a shocked silence put into words, yet it is more eloquent and makes a more impressive effect than any hectic 'operatic dramatics' could be. The 'contemplative' ensemble, as Strauss called it, is truly dramatic.

Thus, although music's tendency to delay appears to endanger its dramatic impact, it is not a weakness that needs to be compensated for in opera by energetic theatrical business, but is closely and inseparably bound up with one ability for dramatic effect that the ordinary spoken play lacks and sometimes seems to desire, if appearances are not deceptive: the ability to give a fleeting moment an unreal duration, and hold it fixed for contemplation. Perhaps, contrary to one popular notion of 'operatic' action, opera comes closest to its ideal at moments, such as the scene on the cathedral steps in *Lohengrin* or the quintet in *Die Meistersinger*, when the action stands still and the music seems to be saying more than the characters know or can express, when the music becomes that 'spirit of the narrative' of which Thomas Mann once spoke.

The tension at the moment of the 'contemplative' ensemble in *Lohengrin*, the conflict between oppressive awareness of the inevitable and the remnants of hope, are expressed in the harmonies and tonal relationships; harmony was more than a formal principle for Wagner, who always, if summarily, stressed its expressive and allegorical nature.

The conclusion of the scene sums it all up: beside the overwhelming fortissimo of the Frageverbot (the theme of Lohengrin's admonition to Elsa not to ask his name), which is stated in F minor, the final chord in C major is a wispy pianissimo: insubstantial, hollow, the major key is quite without conviction. The beginning of the ensemble is no less significant, detached from what has preceded it by an abrupt change of key, from A minor to B♭ major. The absence of harmonic transition creates a formal caesura, an interruption of the musical and the dramatic progress. However, after only a few bars, the B♭ major that appears to be the key of the new ensemble proves to be nothing more than a stepping-stone to C minor. The double function of the B♭ major acts as a fleeting allegory of the nature of the ensemble as a whole, both in its remoteness, its detachment from the course of the action, and in its twilight uncertainty. The harmony is more 'eloquent' than the melody, the actual 'speech' of the music.

The underlying tonality of the ensemble also has a symbolic function; the doubled, or mixed, key of C major–minor is divided, self-contradictory, and in the middle of the nineteenth century may well have been found more confusing than illuminating. However, the major–minor dichotomy is not exploited as a primitive formula, a musical slogan, but is more subtly outlined, with E minor or A minor (keys subsidiary to C major) being used in association with C minor and, vice versa, E♭ major or F minor (keys subsidiary to C minor) being used with C major. C major is not heard explicitly until after its presence has been tacitly assumed as the intermediary between E minor and C minor, whose contrast without an assumption of C major would be incomprehensible, a harmonic blind spot.

The association between the principal keys and their subsidiaries expresses, on the other hand, the paradoxical intermingling of stillness and disquiet which is the dominant characteristic of the ensemble as a whole. Abruptly as the subsidiary tonalities sometimes stand out, they are not stations along a harmonic path, a programme of modulations towards a goal, but merely delineations of the major–minor contrast, to which they lend different colourings. The double key is the compositional prerequisite of the paradoxical simultaneity of restless change and unevolving suspension, it is the scene's allegorical signature; instead of setting off a harmonic progress, something that initially suggests contrast to C minor turns out after a few bars to be a paraphrase of C major, the other partner in the mixed key, and, vice versa, contrast to C major proves a paraphrase of C minor.

4

Given Wagner's ambition to establish or justify his musical tragedy in symphonic terms, and the symphony in terms of tragedy, the musical unity of a music drama is analogous to that of a symphonic movement.

> Nevertheless the new form of dramatic music, if it is also to be a work of art *qua* music, must have...the unity of a symphonic movement, and it achieves that if it extends over the whole drama in the closest possible affinity with it, and not just over separate, arbitrarily selected segments of it.

However, the symphonic form of musical drama, exactly like leitmotivic technique with which it is intimately related, is not subject to any set formula, but has to be recreated according to a new set of principles and means in each new work.

Just as Senta's ballad in *Der fliegende Holländer* provided the starting point of the composition, as the 'unifying thematic image', so in *Lohengrin*, as Wagner explained in the *Communication*, he attempted to realize a similar unity:

> only this time I did not already have a complete musical item like the ballad in front of me, but only first shaped the image, in which the thematic radii came together, out of the construction of the scenes, out of their organic growth one from another, and then allowed it to appear everywhere where it was necessary for the comprehension of the principal situations.

Judging by that, an analysis of *Lohengrin* ought to be able to convert Wagner's metaphor into musical terms and discover the 'image' in which the 'thematic radii' come together.

The number of melodic motives or themes which have a structural role in the inner action conveyed by the music is still very small in *Lohengrin*, compared to the *Ring* (or even *Das Rheingold*). (Motives like the royal fanfares or the musical motto of the Judgement of God, which owe their origin and form to the onstage music, remain peripheral, although they recur often enough: they are musical 'props' and make no contribution to the 'symphonic web'.) Another obvious difference between the motivic technique of *Lohengrin* and the true leitmotivic process first developed in the *Ring* is the retention of regular, 'quadratic' periodic structures, which Wagner later avoided and expressly condemned. The principal motives are all stated initially as complete periods with antecedent and consequent clauses; divergences from this norm are unimportant.

The Grail motive finishes on the dominant instead of on the tonic in the eighth bar – that is, contrary to the rule, it is harmonically open:

The consequent clause of Elsa's motive, which has previously been linked with a different antecedent, seems, in Elsa's motive, to have been tacked on, rather than to develop out of the antecedent:

In Lohengrin's motive the consequent (which it would be supererogatory to quote) is expanded sequentially from four to nine bars, but the quadratic framework is still clearly discernible:

The Frageverbot motive consists of a two–bar phrase repeated and an undivided consequent of four bars:

Ortrud's motive is the other way round, made up of an undivided four-bar antecedent and a repeated two–bar phrase, which does not, however, bring the period to a proper conclusion:

In the course of the work, which forms a 'symphonic web' according to Wagner, the thematic periods are divided up into smaller motivic and structural units, to be restored complete only at the end: a method reminiscent of, and historically dependent on, the symphonic process of development and reprise. Antecedent and consequent clauses are separated from each other, and the motives eventually shrink to short quotations, which are then always ready to be inserted into the musical fabric without strain or technical difficulty, whenever the inner or external action requires it. It is doubtful whether the process can be called reduction, strictly speaking, for these fragments are always of the opening bars of the themes – the motives of the Frageverbot, the Grail and Lohengrin – which constitute the real substance of the whole, the point from which the musical conception takes flight. The thematic periods should be understood as the outcome of elaboration of the motives and not vice versa; the motives are not the result of subdividing the thematic periods. The periodic structure is secondary.

On the other hand, Wagner was not as yet able to escape from the regular syntax of four-bar and eight-bar groups, the scaffolding, the framework without which the music would have broken up into isolated declamatory and arioso phrases. The idea of leitmotivic technique in the stricter sense, the belief that quadratic periodic structure was no longer necessary and could be replaced by musical prose, as soon as a dense network of motivic combinations existed in its place to ensure coherent musical form, was not realized until the *Ring*.

The motives in *Lohengrin* either expand to become thematic periods, or, reduced to short quotations, they stand out as interpolations in the regular periodic structure which provides the compositional framework, making the impression of additions primarily motivated by textual and dramatic considerations, that is by 'exterior' factors. On the other hand, when listened to carefully, the separate motives are always conceptually linked to the thematic periods in which they originated. The fact that they have a formal musical function, and are not just arbitrary insertions but can be grasped as contributory elements in a coherent development, is due to the possibility of referring them back, like the fragments of a thematic group in a symphonic development, to the exposition which they take up and carry through to a conclusion. Presumably it is because the motivic quotations are linked to an exposition in this way, deriving a formal musical purpose in addition to their primary dramatic function, that Wagner spoke of an 'image' in which the 'thematic radii' come together.

5

The categories of 'progressive' and 'conservative' become rather confused when applied to Wagner, with musical factors contradicting dramatic situations. The dialogue between Telramund and Ortrud at the beginning of the second act is musically the most advanced scene in *Lohengrin*, and this is not something that can be written off as accidental; rather it typifies a recurrent dilemma: it is the 'villains', the 'antis', Venus in *Tannhäuser*, Ortrud in *Lohengrin* and Beckmesser in *Meistersinger*, who are presented in exploratory and adventurous musical language. In other words, Wagner, the 'progressive' composer, was compelled by his plots to let musical tradition, the lyric intonation of a Wolfram von Eschenbach or a Walther von Stolzing, have the last word.

At the beginning of Telramund and Ortrud's dialogue the conventional musical structure is still visible: recitatives, only sporadically based on motives of expression or gesture, act as the foil to an aria for Telramund ('Durch dich mußt' ich verlieren'), which is constructed in regular eight-bar periods and does not mark any advance on Lysiart's aria in Act II of *Euryanthe*. The way the scene ends also defers to tradition; indeed, in finales Wagner was almost always inclined to sacrifice stylistic principle to theatrical effect.

But the middle section of the scene (from 'Du wilde Seherin') anticipates the technique of the *Ring*. The vocal melody moves without a break from recitative to arioso and back again, without the stylistic distinctions between the two drawing any attention to themselves. The decisive factor is the rhythmic irregularity: two-bar groups alternate with phrases $1\frac{1}{2}$ or $2\frac{1}{2}$ bars long. Wagner abandons altogether the principle of rhythmic correspondence or complementariness (the formal convention which, when two-bar phrases are added together to make four-bar groups, and four-bar groups to make eight-bar periods, enables the listener to discern the progressive accumulation of units until finally the plastic form of the whole is seen in its entirety); instead phrases are isolated by their irregular lengths. With 'quadratic' rhythm dissolved into 'prose' in this way, and 'open' syntax taking the place of 'closed', the music has to find a compensatory formal basis, and this is the recurrence of motives. The dialogue between Ortrud and Telramund is supported almost throughout by orchestral motives which, together and in conjunction with the vocal phrases, form the 'melody' as Wagner understood the term. Unlike the sporadic quotations in the more 'conservative' dialogue or duet for Lohengrin and Elsa, the motives in this passage – basically Ortrud's motive (which should perhaps be described as a motivic group) supplemented by the Frageverbot theme and a chordal sequence characterizing Ortrud as sorceress (and reminiscent of the 'magic sleep' harmonies of the *Ring*) – are not insertions in the musical text but constitute its substance. It is a model that anticipates one of the essential elements of leitmotivic composition, the technical foundation without which the dramaturgical idea would have remained a utopian fantasy.

Tristan und Isolde

1

With ostentatious simplicity, Wagner called *Tristan* an 'action', not a 'musical drama'. Judged according to the usual concepts, to which, however, it refuses to be subject, it is neither a drama nor a stage epic. The second act, the centre of the work in more than the obvious sense, contains a soundless catastrophe which happens without action and really without words: the colloquy between Tristan and Isolde is so far removed from the antithetical dialogue of traditional drama that it seems almost irrelevant whether the speaker is Tristan or Isolde; the sentences and fragments of sentences are interchangeable, and indeed sometimes are exchanged.

On the other hand, almost every trace of the story's epic origins has been expunged. The large number of episodes narrated by Gottfried von Strassburg in his epic poem is much reduced and their essence is compressed into a few scenes with an energy of concentration that earned the unreserved admiration of a writer like Gottfried Keller, whose own feeling for language was as different from Wagner's as it could be.

When Wagner tried to outline *Tristan* in words, the external action involuntarily shrank to a few sparse allusions, and the inner action emerged as the only important one:

> The loyal vassal, on behalf of his king, wooed Isolde, the woman whom he would not admit to himself he loved, who went with him as his sovereign's bride because she was powerless herself to do anything but follow the wooer. The goddess of love, jealous for her rights that were thus suppressed, took her revenge; she arranges, through an ingenious error, for the young couple to drink the love potion that Isolde's mother has

prudently sent along, according to the custom of the time, for the man with whom her daughter is to make a political marriage. Thanks to the potion their passion suddenly flares up and they have to confess mutually that they belong only to each other. And now there were no bounds to the longing, the desire, the bliss and the anguish of love: the world, power, fame, glory, honour, chivalry, loyalty, friendship, all swept away like chaff, an empty dream; only one thing is left alive: yearning, yearning, insatiable desire, ever reborn – languishing and thirsting; the sole release – death, dying, extinction, never more to wake!

The third act, Tristan's wound, the flight to Kareol and the agonized wait for Isolde – let alone King Marke's forgiveness when he comes to understand – are not even mentioned in this summary. The 'events' that might have been included are thus nothing more than the external enactment of the inner action that has already been concluded in the 'eventless' duologue in the second act: 'the sole release – death, dying, extinction, never more to wake!'

So the 'action' ('Handlung') of *Tristan*'s subtitle is the inner action. It is also a translation of 'drama' ('things to be done'); by using it where one would normally expect to find the Greek word, Wagner makes us stop short and remember the original meaning of an expression that has become threadbare through overfamiliarity. His intention was to show that the inner drama, which is the essential action, is freed in *Tristan* from the encrustation of outer action, the business of events. This return to essentials, as Wagner understood it, is expressed in the translation, which gives its real meaning back to the word 'drama'. Wagner wrote of *Tristan* in 1860 in *The Music of the Future:*

> One look at the size of this poem will show you that that expansive particularity devoted by the poet of a historical subject to the explanation of the outer circumstances of the action, to the detriment of the clear exposition of the inner motivations, I have dared to devote to the latter alone...The whole gripping action only materializes because the innermost soul demands it, and it appears before us in the shape given it from within.

One important point: in drama of the modern age, at least, dialogue is effectively the medium of the action, yet this is something Wagner ignored or failed to recognize when he sought to explain *Tristan* as the quintessence of an 'action', meaning 'drama'. The work does not lack dramatic dialectical argument; the substance specifically of the colloquy in the second act is dialectical. But it develops contrary to the norms of drama, not in dialogue, not between the characters, but within them, as an inner process common to them both.

2

The love potion still has an active part to play in Gottfried's poem, though even there it is not taken altogether seriously; but in Wagner it is primarily a symbol, though an enigmatic one: a dialectical puzzle. Plainly – and there has never been any confusion on this point – unlike the fatal potion in *Götterdämmerung* it changes nothing but simply brings into the open something which already exists but has not previously been admitted. It is more difficult to disentangle the dialectics of the two potions, of love and death, which amounts to rather more than the simple fact of their being exchanged by Brangäne, the half-guilty, half-innocent tool of fate. It is the belief that it is the death potion that leads Tristan and Isolde to drink the love potion, but the mistake is an instrument of the truth; appearance and essence, love potion and death potion, enter a twilight area in which they become virtually indistinguishable. The drink is a love potion only insofar as it is believed to be a death potion: because Isolde and Tristan have drunk death they confess to each other a love about which they would otherwise have kept silent, plainly though they themselves knew of its existence.

If it is a yearning for death which is turned into love by the drink, it was from love that the yearning for death previously grew. Death was Tristan's and Isolde's only way of escape from a doomed love. The earlier events in their story are full of violence. Tristan killed Morold, the Irish champion betrothed to Isolde, cut off his head and sent it to Isolde in a gesture of brutal arrogance. But he had been mortally wounded himself by Morold's poisoned sword, and had to turn to Isolde as the only person who could heal him. At first going under an assumed name, he was later recognized, and Isolde, though convinced of her duty to kill him, found herself unable to do it.

> Von seinem Bette
> blickt' er her –
> nicht auf das Schwert,

nicht auf die Hand –
er sah mir in die Augen.
Seines Elendes
jammerte mich;
das Schwert – das ließ ich fallen.

'*He looked up from his bed – not at the sword, not at my hand – he looked into my eyes. His miserable plight won my pity; the sword – I let it fall.*'

But if this means that their love reaches back to the time of Tristan's first voyage to Ireland, then it seems contradictory that, after his return to Cornwall, Tristan persuaded King Marke to woo Isolde. What does Tristan's 'betrayal' mean? In the second act they talk of the treachery and delusion of the daytime, the code of honour and custom which deceived Tristan. But the difference in rank – the assumption that honour and custom required the vassal to know his station – is too weak a motive to explain Tristan's tragic error. The tragedy of duty dominated the theatre from the sixteenth century to the early nineteenth, but *Tristan* has outgrown its conventions.

The love of Tristan and Isolde, a love driving them into the arms of death, is an open secret. Isolde acknowledges it at the beginning of the drama, without a potion to make her say the words:

Mir erkoren –
mir verloren –
hehr und heil,
kühn und feig:
Todgeweihtes Haupt!
Todgeweihtes Herz!

'*Elect to me – lost to me – sublime and without blemish, dauntless and a coward: head sacred to death, heart sacred to death!*'

Tristan keeps his own counsel:

Des Schweigens Herrin
heißt mich schweigen:
fass' ich, was sie verschwieg,
verschweig' ich, was sie nicht faßt.

'*The mistress of silence bids me keep silent: if I comprehend what she veils in silence, I will keep silent about what she does not comprehend.*'

What he veils in silence is nothing less than that both his instincts and his mind recognize the love that binds him and Isolde to each other as destiny. The 'Frau Minne' to whom they refer in their colloquy in the second act is not an allegory of a state of mind or soul, but a goddess who delivers Tristan up to a fate that he cannot escape. Again and again, every step he takes in the hope of escaping only enmeshes him more. Separating himself from Isolde, by wooing her on King Marke's behalf, brings him more painfully close to her; the poison which he expects to release him turns into the love potion which brings the inescapable into the open; and although, when King Marke discovers him with Isolde, he throws himself on the sword of Melot who betrayed him, he cannot die but has to wait for Isolde, in the grip of a longing that is nothing but torment. The shepherd's 'traurige Weise' in the third act is Tristan's true leitmotiv. But Isolde knows what he will not say, and says it.

> Doch ach! Dich täuschte
> der falsche Trank,
> daß dir von neuem
> die Nacht versank;
> dem einzig am Tode lag,
> den gab er wieder dem Tag.

> *' But ah! the false drink made you believe that night was falling for you once again; you were intent only on death, but the drink gave you back to day.'*

The myth of Tristan and Isolde's love as something perfect in itself, disturbed only by outside forces, is a misconception rooted in blind enthusiasm.

3

In 1872, in an essay disowning the expression 'music drama', Wagner defined his 'dramas' as 'deeds of music which have become visible'. The metaphor, encompassing an entire theory, seems to contradict the earlier thesis, developed in *Opera and Drama*, that in the 'drama of words-and-music' ('Wort-Ton-Drama') the music is one of the means of expression available to the drama. At all events, those who construed the history of opera as the alternation of hegemony between 'words' and 'music' took it as an admission of the primacy of music. Anyone who was looking for biographical premises could attribute the reasons for this profound change – insofar as it was one – on the one hand to Wagner's experiences in composing *Tristan* and on the other to the influence of Schopenhauer, in whose metaphysics of music (crudely summarized) the visible world of phenomena is demoted to a mere reflection of the 'will', which has its being in music.

The thesis that the music took precedence in the composition of *Tristan* also appears to be supported by some of the documents of the period of its gestation. In 1854, three years before he even wrote the text, Wagner told Liszt: 'I have drafted a *Tristan und Isolde* in my head, the simplest but most full-blooded musical conception; at the end, when the black flag is flying, I shall cover myself with it – to die.' There are two significant points in this: first that he speaks of a 'musical conception', not a poetic one; and secondly the mention of the 'black flag', which belongs to the part played in the legend by Isolde of the White Hands (who does not appear at all in Wagner). In other words, the idea Wagner had in his head in 1854 was still a very long way from the final version, and appears to be a basic musico-poetic idea still lacking the precise form of the later text. In November 1856 he wrote to Marie Wittgenstein that while working on *Siegfried* he had slipped 'unawares into *Tristan*': 'music without words for the present. There are some places, too, where I shall very likely do the music before the words.' And early in 1857 he sent Mathilde Wesendonk some music from *Tristan* without any words.

It is not altogether clear how the fact that musical motives played an active part in the conception of *Tristan* from the beginning, side by side with poetic ones, constitutes proof of musical primacy. (The chronological factor is not important: the texts of eighteenth-century operas were written before the music, but that does not affect the fact that they were aesthetically secondary.) Above all, it is obvious that the problem of musical drama, as Wagner saw it, has been distorted by being formulated in terms of 'words versus music'.

The common assumption is that in *Opera and Drama* Wagner drew up a theory of the precedence of the text over the music, which he then put into practice in the *Ring*; but the appearance is deceptive and arises from the erroneous equation of 'text' with 'drama'. (The error is all the more incomprehensible since even in a spoken play the text is not the whole of the drama.) Wagner's postulate that the music must be one of the means at the drama's service loses all reasonable sense if the reader understands nothing by the word 'drama' but 'text', and derives from *Opera and Drama* nothing but a threadbare theory subordinating the music to the text. In Wagner's vocabulary 'drama' is the outcome of the conjunction of text, music and stage action; the text, no more and no less than the music, is one of the means serving the drama.

> If the poetic intention is still discernible as such, it is because it has not been fully subsumed, that is realized, in the composer's expression; on the other hand, if the composer's expression is still recognizable as such, it is because it has not been completely permeated by the poetic intention; only when the expression has surrendered its individual, particular identity in the realization of that intention do both intention and expression cease to exist, and the reality to which both aspired is achieved: that reality is the drama, in the performance of which we should no longer be conscious of either intention or expression, being overwhelmed by its content, as an action of which we instinctively acknowledge the necessary human truth.

The 'intention', the initial and underlying concept of a musical drama, first takes shape in the text, it is true, as what Wagner called the 'poetic intention' ('die dichterische Absicht'); but it is to the music that it owes its 'realization' for the region of perception that has no need of words. The drama can proceed, according to Wagner's dogma, only from the musical realization.

Of course the definition of drama, twenty years later, as a 'deed of music which has become visible' lays more stress on the importance of the music, which Schopenhauer had invested with greater metaphysical dignity; but the difference between music, as that which enables the drama to proceed out of the 'poetic intention' by 'realizing' it, and music, whose relationship to drama is that of instigation to achievement, is very far from being a fundamental contradiction. In any case, Wagner himself was not primarily concerned with whether the music was subordinate to the text in musical drama or vice versa; but if readers bring to a theoretical text a question that it was not originally asking, it is hardly the fault of the text if the answer they find there seems confused or contradictory.

Contrary to the fantasies of some historians, *Tristan* does not represent a return to 'opera', even to some utopian ideal of opera. The notion that the text is taken up into the music, or even the drama into the 'orchestral symphony', is a fable, born of enthusiastic but imprecise listening. The text and the music are not simply equal in importance, which is a truism, but their relationship in some places is better described as intercutting, rather than one of correspondence or mutual absorption.

The first part of the colloquy in the second act, the lover's jubilation at being together again, expressed in emphatic fragmentary clauses, breaks off at the words 'ewig, ewig ein'. What follows ('Wie lange fern') is a passage of reflection, as they muse on the experience of proximity as distance and distance as proximity in antithetical images and formulas. The switch in the dialogue is almost disconcertingly apparent, which makes it all the more obvious that Wagner did not attempt to match it in the music. The development of the motive that has dominated the first part, one the exegetes have identified as the expression of love's exultancy or have simply labelled 'Love theme', is carried on after the turning point in the text.

The new beginning and the end of the old interlock, the text changes direction abruptly, while the 'symphonic web' continues as before. It is not that the music is in any way 'absolute', proceeding regardless of the break: the love theme is darkened chromatically and inclines towards diminuendo instead of crescendo, as if the shadow of Isolde's reflective mood is also cast over the jubilation of reunion; but it is another nine bars before the musical motive that primarily characterizes this second 'paragraph' of the text is introduced, and this time it is the text that proceeds uninterrupted, bridging the musical caesura. (There is no need to repeat the analysis, but the same process recurs at the next caesura in the dialogue, at Isolde's words 'Im Dunkel du, im Lichte ich'.)

The interlocking or intercutting in the relationship of the text and the music is not accident, let alone incompetence, but a typically Wagnerian concept of form. The music is no more subordinate to the structure of the text, a mere illustration of it, than the text is a vehicle for the music, an excuse for its development; rather, the music and the text, the articulation of the motives and of the dialogue, interlock in order to put into practice a principle that Wagner called the 'art of transition' and believed to be his 'most refined and profound art'.

4

It was in a letter to Mathilde Wesendonk of 29 October 1859 that Wagner aired the subject of the 'art of transition'.

> I have come to detest the abrupt, the brusque; it is often unavoidable and necessary, but even then it should not occur without the mood having been so determinedly prepared for the sudden transition that it actually demands the change of itself. My greatest masterpiece in the art of the most refined, gradual transition is undoubtedly the great scene in the second act of *Tristan und Isolde*. The beginning of the scene offers life, pressed down and running over in the most turbulent emotion – the ending, the most solemn, intensely felt longing for death. Those are the cornerposts: now just you take a look, my dear, at how I've connected them, how it leads over from one to the other! There you have the secret of my musical form, of which I dare to claim that nobody has ever dreamt of anything with such full agreement of every part and extended so clearly, accommodating every detail, over such a large span.

There is more to the 'secret of the musical form' than the fact that the musical motives, like the emotions they express, merge into one another uninterruptedly, without discernible rifts in the symphonic web. If analysis is to go beyond motivic exegesis it should perhaps explore what is meant by 'mediation' in terms of the musical form.

An outline analysis of the dialogue between Isolde and Tristan in Act I, Scene 5, will give some indication of what might be learned (the associations in the central scene of the second act spread over too wide a span to make it a practicable proposition here). The opening period clearly takes a ternary form, $A^1 B A^2$ (18, 12 and 12 bars). But the (varied) reprise, A^2, which concludes the first, ternary period, is simultaneously the beginning, X^1, of a second, binary period, $X^1 X^2$ (14 and 11 bars). The disposition of the motives in the second period ('Begehrt, Herrin, was ihr wünscht') is, at first sight, confused:

	X^1				X^2		
motives	*a*	*b*	*a*	*c*	*d*	*b*	*e*	*d*
number of bars	2	2	3	4	3	2	5	4

The only motives common to both X^1 and X^2 are b and d. But, since b is a subdivision of the motivic complex $a\ b$, it is impossible not to hear the analogy between the two beginnings.

It is the motives a and c that distinguish X^1 and X^2. On the other hand, it is precisely a and c that relate X^1, in its function as A^2, to A^1. So it would be wrong to run the periods $A^1\ B\ A^2$ and $X^1\ X^2$ together into a single scheme, $A^1\ B\ A^2\ A^3$; although the identity of A^2 and X^1 relates the two periods to each other, they are separated by the fact that different elements enable the 'equivocal' section to function as A^2 on the one hand and X^1 on the other. (In other words, A^1 and X^2 have nothing in common and therefore cannot be designated by A^1 and A^3.)

The form is 'closed' and 'open' at one and the same time: 'closed' because it provides binary and ternary schemata, the basic patterns of formal tradition ($A^1\ B\ A^2$ and $X^1\ X^2$); 'open' because the components do not follow cleanly one after another, but interpenetrate, so that their delimitations become uncertain. In the 'equivocal' section (A^2/X^1), motive c marks the end of A^2 (analogous to A^1), but motive d completes X^1 (corresponding to X^2); thus the section has two endings, that pertaining to each of its functions being different from the other. And because the formal components are ambiguous in their functions or run into each other, in the theatre, when they are heard as imprecisely as they almost inevitably are, they create the impression of something blurred, even amorphous. But this appearance of 'formlessness' is in reality the outcome of the utmost formal differentiation.

The same formal idea – it is a consciously adopted principle, not an accidental discovery – is the basis of the exchange between Tristan and Isolde ('Wohin nun Tristan scheidet') at the end of the second act, after Tristan's reply, which is really a kind of silence, to Marke's reproaches. In broad outline, the dialogue is in five sections (14, 16, 18, 12 and 18 bars), the formal unity of which derives from the third and fifth, Tristan's strophe and Isolde's only minimally different antistrophe. The relationship between the first three sections is vexing for formal analysts who prefer theory to be observed to the letter. The third seems in some respects to be a conflation of the first and second: its opening is the same as that of the second ('Dem Land, das Tristan meint' and 'Was, da sie mich gebar'); on the other hand, the first section, a complex of four motives, returns, though not completely unchanged, to furnish the middle part and the close of the third section ('das bietet dir Tristan'). The first section is introductory in nature, and at first the second and third appear to be an arioso strophe and antistrophe. But the difference in the continuation and the third section's reversion to the first confuse the initial impression of the form, without expunging it. The subsequent impression of the form is of a first schema (A B^1 B^2: introduction, strophe and antistrophe) interlocking with a second (A^1 B A^2: exposition, middle section and reprise). Formal models, which would appear to be mutually exclusive, are compelled to form a paradoxical unity.

5

The practice of giving Wagnerian leitmotive names which fix an identity to them once and for all is as questionable as it is unavoidable: questionable, because the translation of musical expression into precise verbal terms is never satisfactory; unavoidable, because the idea of wordless, instinctive understanding of musical motives, without the need for mediation through language, is an illusion. The name that half-misses the object altogether is nevertheless the only way to get at it. But in order to have a clear view of the ramificatory meanings a motive can have, one must start with a basic idea and gradually differentiate it; the infinite wealth of instinctive understanding at which Wagner aimed does not come into existence at the first impact of immediacy, but – if at all – at the second stage, when immediacy has combined with reflection.

Thus the uncertainty over nomenclature – whether one motive is better called 'Tristan' or 'Destiny', or another the 'Potion of Reconciliation' or 'Fate' – is not a matter that would be solved by more exact exegesis, but is the reflection and consequence of one of the characteristics of leitmotivic technique itself. T. W. Adorno's criticism of the technique, which starts from the premiss that the names given to the motives identify their essence (rather than being imposed on them from without), is itself wide of the mark. Adorno chooses to blame Wagner because a motive, which aspires to be the spontaneous, unrepeatable expression of an emotional state, is reduced by the name it bears to a minor allegorical image. (The problem of the musical repetition of an expression that is essentially unrepeatable is not peculiar to Wagner but common to all music before Schoenbergian expressionism, and can therefore be ignored here.)

There are two considerations here, which need to be kept separate. There is no denying the presence in *Tristan* of allegorical musical motives, though they are less prominent than in the *Ring*; but they are not emotive

expressions that have been transformed and, so to speak, frozen by reason
of their allegorical significance. In Wagner allegorical motives are to be
found side by side with emotive ones, and it is not always possible to
draw sharp distinctions between them. The motives associated with
death and day are primarily musical allegories and provide an analogy
to the allegorical tendency of the text.

It is not by chance that, since Hans von Wolzogen first traced his 'clues',
there has never been any dispute over the denomination of these two
motives. By contrast, in the case of those motives of undeniably
expressive character which are grouped round the central elements of
the inner action – the yearning for love and for death, which is the same
yearning – the nomenclature has always been uncertain. (If a triumphant
solution were found, it would involve an allegorization of the emotions.)
The ambiguities of the emotions resist identification in rigid terms.

Just as the meaning of a motive can be indefinite, or can branch out
to cover a field of related meanings, so too the musical shapes can
fluctuate. They are more variable than in the *Ring*, and the frontier
between fully-fledged leitmotive and what Ernst Kurth dubbed 'developmental motives' – half-amorphous musical figures that have their
being in the subordinate parts – is fluid. Not only are motives related
to one another – the Suffering motive is an inversion of the Yearning
motive, and Marke's motive, at least at the outset, is an inversion of
Tristan's

– but they also blend into one another and are finally lost in shapeless intangibility. It might be appropriate to compare the motives in *Tristan* – as distinct from those in the *Ring* – with the threads in a woven fabric that come to the surface, disappear and divide, rather than with building blocks that are placed beside and above each other.

There is a greater degree of mutual interdependence between the melodic writing – the musical sense of the motives and their expressive character – and the harmony, the chord structure, in *Tristan* than in the *Ring*. The Yearning motive, the trademark of the style of *Tristan*, would be an amorphous and almost meaningless sequence of notes – a section of a chromatic scale – without the chords that support and determine the melody. The harmony, the '*Tristan* chord', acquires motivic significance.

On the other hand, the chordal structure is almost inconceivable without the Suffering motive, the contrapuntal subordinate part underlying the Yearning motive in the top line. The harmonic writing is supported and motivated by the melodic writing in exactly the same way as the melody owes its significance and colouring to the harmony. Explaining the motives as the chord structure 'composed out', or the chord structure as the outcome of the conjunction of motives, gives a distorted, because one-sided, view. The elements interlock and inter-react in such a way that there is nothing to be gained from the attempt to distinguish which is primary and which secondary.

Similarly, the Fate motive (or the motive of the potion of reconciliation) does not owe its unmistakable, distinctive character to the melody as such, but to the association with a sequence of chords which poses a musical puzzle: disconcerting and yet compelling.

The harmony is not self-justifying (on paper, in the abstract, the sequence of chords would be meaningless) but grows out of the relationship between the Fate motive, as the lower part, and a chromatic counterpoint, which is to some degree part of the motive, so that one is driven to speak paradoxically of a 'polyphonic motive'.

But the fact that the chordal association is not self-sufficient but partly, even primarily, founded in the motives means that the tradition of tonality, of tonal harmony, is, if not suspended, at least endangered in *Tristan*. For tonality, the ruling principle in music from the seventeenth century to the nineteenth, is nothing other than a self-justifying system of chordal relationships, independent of melodic or contrapuntal processes. It is not that Wagner anticipated Schoenbergian atonality; there was never any question of his abandoning the principle of tonality, and he used to attribute emotive and symbolic significances to tonal relationships. Yet the harmonies of *Tristan* point the way that was to lead eventually to the dissolution of tonality, the emancipation of melody and counterpoint from preformed chordal associations. *Tristan* is a primary source in the history of modern music.

Die Meistersinger von Nürnberg

1

Die Meistersinger is the brainchild of an untrustworthy sense of humour. (Wagner complained that Liszt and Nietzsche did not like his jokes.) Beneath the surface of the German idyll, set among crooked alleys filled with the intoxicating scents of elder trees, there is a strain of violence. The populace that assembles in the third act to hymn the praise of the Reformation and 'holy German art' is the same that in the second fills the streets with a riot, triggered off by an occasion so trivial that its true causes can only lie all the deeper. (The fact that when Wagner conceived the scene he was drawing on something he had himself experienced in Nuremberg is without relevance to the completed work.) Walther von Stolzing, the Prometheus-figure of a 'new art' that triumphs over the outmoded, fossilized rules of the guild of mastersingers, is in other respects a tearaway, hand ever on sword to deal with any hindrance in his path, even the nightwatchman. It is not so surprising that the citizens of Nuremberg regard him with distrust. Sixtus Beckmesser, the principal opponent and censor of innovation, a venomous pedant but, for all that, a humanist in the sixteenth-century sense and a holder of high civic office, seems to be bewitched, forever falling into absurd plights where he only looks grotesque. And Hans Sachs, who rises, nobly resigned, above the frets of other men, has another face. The malicious tricks he plays on Beckmesser recall Wotan's wagering with Mime, where the wager is a trap. Just as Wotan leaves it to Siegfried to exact the forfeit Mime owes, so Sachs delivers up Beckmesser to the lethal derision of the crowd. (For both Wotan and Sachs, resignation involves keeping their own hands clean.) The C major jubilation of the close of the work, after everything that has come before it, is not so serene, after all, to an ear that has been tuned musico-dramatically. It is no accident that the motive that blends with the final chord is that to which the crowd mocked Beckmesser.

Wagner first sketched a scenario for the work in 1845, when he was conductor at the royal opera in Dresden. It was a decade and a half later, after the completion of *Tristan*, that he returned to it, wrote a new scenario and worked out the text in the winter of 1861–2, while living in Paris. Yet it seems that he had been mulling it over half-subconsciously during the long interval, because the 1851 *Communication to my Friends* includes a description of the plot which has already moved on in some respects from the original sketch.

> Just as a comic satyr play followed the tragedy in the Athenian theatre, so I suddenly had the idea of a comedy that could follow my 'Singers' War at Wartburg' as a truly relevant satyr play. It was the 'Mastersingers of Nuremberg' with Hans Sachs at their head.

The plot owed some of its basic threads to Lortzing's *Hans Sachs*, but there was an important difference in the prominence given to questions of aesthetics.

> I conceived of Hans Sachs as the last manifestation of the artistically creative spirit of the ordinary people

– Wagner evidently derived this idea from Jacob Grimm –

> and contrasted him in this role with the petty bourgeoisie of the mastersingers, whose utterly ludicrous pedantry, poetry-by-tabulature

– of which Wagner, the literary scholar among librettists, had made a thorough study in Wagenseil's *Nürnberger Chronik* –

> I embodied in the figure of the 'Marker'.

(This was not yet an allusion to Hanslick; he was cast as Beckmesser, the Marker or musical censor, only later, when he had become a critic of Wagner.)

> The oldest member of the guild

– later Pogner, whom 'God has made a rich man' –

has offered the hand of his young daughter to whichever master should win the prize in a public singing contest that is about to take place. The Marker, who is already a suitor for the girl, now finds he has a rival in the person of a young man of knightly birth, who is moved by his reading of epic poetry and the old minnesingers to leave the crumbling castle and empty coffers of his ancestors and come to Nuremberg to learn the art of mastersong

– which regarded itself as the continuation and codification of knightly Minnesang.

He applies to join the guild, spurred on to do so by his having fallen head over heels in love with the girl who is offered as prize.

(Love is always at first sight in Wagner.)

Asked to submit a test-piece, he sings enthusiastically in praise of women, but the Marker's objections to the song are so numerous that the candidate is already adjudged to have failed by the time he is halfway through it. Sachs, who has taken to the young man, then – in the knight's own interests – foils his desperate attempt to elope with the girl.

The complication of Sachs's own affection for Eva and his renunciation of her is absent from both the 1845 and 1851 sketches. If *Die Meistersinger* was first conceived as a satyr play to follow *Tannhäuser*, by 1861–2 its closeness to *Tristan* is evident. Sachs renounces Eva so as not to share the fate of King Marke, and says as much. In the 1851 sketch, his plans to thwart Beckmesser are more deliberate. Not only does he disrupt the serenade at Eva's window with 'Jerum, jerum' and noisy hammering, but he gives Beckmesser 'a poem by the young knight, pretending that he does not know where it came from'. (In the eventual version the poem comes into Beckmesser's hands half through theft on his own part, half as a gift intended to trap him.)

But he warns him to take great care in finding a suitable 'Weise' to sing it to. The conceited Marker has every confidence in himself on that score, and then goes and sings the poem before the assembled jury of the masters and the general public to a totally unsuitable tune that quite distorts it

– in the finished work he distorts the text as well –

   so that once again

– as with his serenade –

> he fails. Furious, he accuses Sachs of saddling him with a
> disgraceful poem in order to trick him; the latter declares that
> there is nothing wrong with the poem, but it needs to be sung
> to an appropriate tune. It is agreed that whoever knows the right
> tune shall be the winner. The young knight accomplishes this
> and wins the bride, but spurns the offer of election to the guild.
> Thereupon Sachs makes a humorous defence of the guild and
> its art, concluding with the couplet:
>
> Zerging' das Heil'ge Römische Reich in Dunst,
> Uns bliebe doch die heil'ge deutsche Kunst.
>
> *'If the Holy Roman Empire disappeared in smoke, we should still
> have holy German art.'*

Nietzsche's tenet that art is the only thing that justifies life – or
'delusion' ('Wahn') as Wagner, the disciple of Schopenhauer, called it
– summarizes the theme of *Die Meistersinger*.

   2

   The philosophy of art informing *Die Meistersinger* is in fact more
complex than it at first appears to be, particularly in the relationship
between what is explicit and what remains unsaid. Dramatically, the
foreground is occupied by the confrontation between Beckmesser on the
one hand and Sachs and Walther on the other, but philosophically this
confrontation is almost irrelevant: Beckmesser does not represent any
sector of art, not even mastersong, of which Sachs is the true representative; the Marker is nothing but a caricature of a critic. His role in
the action is allegorical: his jealousy of Walther the 'natural genius', the
shoddiness of his nocturnal serenade and his inability to appreciate or
perform Walther's Prize Song are theatrical symbols for some of the most
popular prejudices against critics, which Wagner unceremoniously
adopted: the assumptions that critics are probably motivated by envy
and are themselves creatively sterile and unable to understand anything
new that departs from the well-worn paths sanctioned by recognized
rules. (Since Wagner's day the situation seems to have been virtually

reversed, with those critics of any importance championing the new, while the public prefers the familiar; but the principal feature of hostility towards criticism, the distrust of responses based on intellectual consideration, remains unaltered, save in its object: the charge of mechanical soullessness is levelled today at new music, not old.)

Beckmesser is no mastersinger: the Mastersingers' theme that launches the prelude could not be less Beckmesserish. Although the conflict of views between Sachs and Beckmesser dominates the stage it is peripheral to the action, while the crucial issues are, if anything, concealed rather than represented dramatically. Sachs may be, in the words of the 1851 outline, 'the last manifestation of the artistically creative spirit of the ordinary people' – the humanist intellectual Beckmesser disparages him on those very grounds – but he is also the living justification of the guild and its rulebook, and it is as their representative that he confronts Walther, because an understanding of the rules is one of the preconditions of artistic mastery, in the possession of which Wagner felt himself secure by 1860, after completing *Tristan*. Sachs, rooted in ancient, popular tradition yet occupying the heights of a conscious and self-confident art, is the dramatic embodiment of a cherished idea of romantic philosophy: the belief that spontaneous 'natural poetry' and 'classicism', early wellsprings of inspiration and late perfection, are essentially one and the same thing. Hans Sachs is Wagner's self-portrait as a classicist.

But this conscious portrayal of Wagner's private idea of himself is opposed by an unacknowledged, subversive and secret idea. In Walther's Trial Song – which arouses the Marker's professional fury, without its being very clear precisely why – Wagner covertly betrays the secret that lies at the heart of his own work. The idea of Walther's 'natural genius' is an illusion, revealed as sham by the Trial Song itself, for its line and rhyme schemes are so complicated that the ability to compose a song to them as immaculately as Walther does presupposes the most intense effort and application. The paradox is not, of course, an accidental oversight on Wagner's part; rather, it encapsulates the esoteric artistic philosophy of *Die Meistersinger*, as opposed to the exoteric philosophy represented by Sachs, to say nothing of the confrontations between Beckmesser and Walther or Sachs. Wagner's fundamental aesthetic conviction, which he shared with Kant, was that art, in order to be art, must conceal itself and appear in the guise of nature. The means and expedients must not be allowed to be visible, reflection must be transformed into spontaneity, immediacy must be recreated and still be

immediacy, and every trace of effort must be expunged. The paradox is
that it takes technique to deny technique. But in Walther the contradictions are resolved in a utopian image: artistry is his natural lot, he
improvises what can only be achieved by reflection. The recreated,
second immediacy, for which Wagner worked so hard, comes to Walther
first time round. And Sachs, thinking about Walther's Trial Song,
describes the effect that Wagner's music, by his own deliberate efforts,
had on his contemporaries:

> Ich fühl's – und kann's nicht verstehn:
> kann's nicht behalten – doch auch nicht vergessen;
> und fass' ich es ganz, kann ich's nicht messen.
>
> *'I feel it – and can't understand it; can't retain it – nor forget it
> either; and if I grasp it entirely, I can't take its measure.'*

3

When it took possession of Wagner in the autumn of 1861, the
idea of *Die Meistersinger* was already a total musico-dramatic conception.
It would be inappropriate and dogmatic to unravel the close interlocking
relationship of textual and musical elements in order to construct a
scheme of priorities in support of some theory of either opera or music
drama. There was neither a pre-existing text that Wagner set to music,
nor music that he then provided with a text. The evidence concerning
the origins and writing of *Die Meistersinger* will be found confused and
contradictory, unless one abandons the attempt to force from it an answer
to the wrong question, that about the precedence of text or music. (The
thesis of the chronological precedence of the music, which, without
further ceremony and with questionable logic, is then made to stand as
proof of objective primacy, is apologetic in intention; it is meant to
defend music drama against the charge of musical formlessness, when
the only valid defence is formal analysis.)

When Wagner decided to carry out his sixteen-year-old project, he
was on a brief visit to Venice in late autumn and in a mood of deep
dejection – the contrast could hardly be more extreme. During the
journey back to Vienna, he wrote in *Mein Leben*,

> *Die Meistersinger*, the text of which I still had in my mind only
> according to my earliest concept, took hold of me, first of all
> as a musical idea; instantaneously and with the greatest clarity,
> I conceived the principal section of the overture in C major.

But one of the C major themes (the guild march, which Ernest Newman calls the King David fanfare), came from Wagenseil's *Nürnberger Chronik*, which Wagner did not study until several months later. In a letter to Mathilde Wesendonk of December 1861, Wagner expressed the matter less emphatically than in *Mein Leben*: 'Something lingered in my mind now, like an overture to a "Mastersingers of Nuremberg".' But what mattered was not whether the fragments he conceived were clearly formed or still fluid, but that he had found the right 'tone' for the work he now wanted to write, the tone that would govern both the text and the musical realization. It is not putting it too strongly to interpret the C major of which he wrote in *Mein Leben* as standing for the quintessence of the world of dignified marches and archaizing counterpoint characteristic of *Die Meistersinger*.

Having sketched the beginning of the overture in November 1861, Wagner wrote the whole piece out in February or March 1862, before a single line of the text had been set – contrary to the norm in operatic composition. The 'thematic image' of the whole work – Senta's ballad in *Der fliegende Holländer* – is in *Die Meistersinger* the overture, a piece of instrumental music. (The form is that of a symphonic poem after the Lisztian pattern. The four movements of classical symphonic form are compressed into a single movement, to whose four parts – first subject, second subject, development and reprise – Wagner gives the character of the various movements of the conventional symphony: Allegro, Andante, Scherzo and Finale.)

The text had been written in the intervening months, December 1861 and January 1862, though it was to undergo later modifications. Nothing shows more clearly than the alternation between drafting music and drafting text that Wagner had started with a conception, the musical and textual elements of which cannot be separated unequivocally into 'first' and 'later'. It was precisely the certainty of the total musico-dramatic idea that made possible the simultaneous conception of text and music; the separation of the two processes is only a matter of appearances.

This could be pursued by reference even to details. The second subject of the overture, the E major melody, standing for the slow movement, was later adopted as the final section (the Abgesang) of Walther's Prize Song. A lack of agreement between the declamation and the phrasing of the line 'in himmlisch neu verklärter Pracht' betrays that the text was written after the music. (It is out of the question that when Wagner composed this part of the overture in February or March 1862 he had in mind the text he had just written: for the text specifically of the Prize Song was completely rewritten later, and not even the metre of the first version is the same.

in himm-lisch neu ver-klär-ter Pracht—

But the theme itself is the representation, the musical substance, of something that was never in any doubt: the words and details of the text may have come later; the dramatic significance was inherent in the theme from the first.

4

Die Meistersinger is the only one of Wagner's works, apart from *Rienzi*, in which it is essential to the plot that it takes place at a particular time in history, not in an undatable mythical or legendary era. (The setting of *Lohengrin* in tenth-century Antwerp is background, not essence: there is nothing to prevent the designer from giving us a Gothic minster; but Nuremberg in the sixteenth century is part of the fabric of *Die Meistersinger*.) The historical element is not just a piece of a dead past, but appears in the role of the prehistory of the present day, as if there were a collective memory reaching back into the sixteenth century. The music sounds like something quoted from memory: it is near and yet remote.

For Wagner, and the nineteenth century in general, 'early music' meant the music of Bach and Handel. (It has only been in the twentieth century that, as contemporary music has introduced ever faster and more startling innovations, the knowledge of earlier music has spread ever further back in time.) If a historical model were sought for the ambience conveyed by the Mastersingers' theme, it could well be the *gravitas* of the slow sections in Bach's French overtures: Wagner's 'old German' style echoes an international or French style. The work is, however, very far from the kind of musical history painting which was one of the aberrations of the nineteenth century.

The historical Hans Sachs's song acclaiming the Reformation, 'Wach' auf, es nahet gen dem Tag', was set by Wagner as it stood. The melody he gave it is not a chorale translated into the musical language of the nineteenth century (it was attempts at such translation that gave rise to the archaism that filled Protestant hymnbooks) but a cantilena that never for a moment denies the age in which it was written and yet seems to contain in itself a recollection of the past. 'It sounded so old and yet was so new': the paradox Sachs ponders, bewildered by Walther's Trial Song, applies to the music of *Die Meistersinger* as a whole.

The infusion of archaism in modernity, the impression, however vague, of something immemoriably old, can be described in technical musical terms. In progressive harmonic writing of the nineteenth century (of which the harmony of *Tristan* is paradigmatic), the increasing complexity of dissonance treatment – which led in the twentieth century to Arnold Schoenberg's 'emancipation of dissonance' from the obligation to resolve – was closely connected with a tendency to chromaticization of chords, to 'colouring' individual notes by raising or lowering them a semitone. The more dissonances a piece of music contained the more chromatic it was. Yet one of the characteristics of the style of *Die Meistersinger* – and perhaps the most important of them – is that, while the dissonance treatment is prominent, the chromaticism is repressed: that is what creates the impression of the old in the new. The opening bars of 'Wach' auf' are typical of the interlocking of the elements.

The process of delaying the resolution of seventh chords (on 'gen' and 'Tag') by inserting intermediate chords is undoubtedly modern, but creates an archaic effect at the same time insofar as, for one thing, there is no chromaticism – the essentially modern element – and, for another, the interpolations give rise to sequences of chords which are unusual in tonal harmony and recall an earlier kind of music, in which the sequence of chords was not yet regulated by tonal norms.

The contrast between old and new is an element in the plot of *Die Meistersinger*, embodied in the rivalry of Beckmesser and Walther, but it becomes confused in the musical realization. It is true that Beckmesser's creative efforts – the serenade and the mangled Prize Song – are given some obvious outmoded characteristics; mechanical coloratura, modal melodies and perfunctory accompaniment, limited to a few chords and figurations on a lute, represent the essence of the musically obsolete, which Wagner equated with meagreness. (The direction of musical progress, he believed, was towards ever greater abundance.) On the other hand, Walther's Prize Song is anything but 'new' music. It is not that it is the spontaneous cantilena that the inattentive listener may take it for: the impression of a flowing cantabile is rather the outcome of an extremely complex method of linking melodic phrases together. (The broad sweep of the music results from painstaking work on the details.) But in the second half of the nineteenth century 'new' music was not cantabile but descriptive, and the supreme example of stylistically advanced, descriptive music in *Die Meistersinger* is the third-act panto-mime for Beckmesser the traditionalist: music which treats musical tradition, or its remnants, as cavalierly as the plot treats Beckmesser the censor.

Archaizing music is 'sentimental' in Schiller's sense of the word: not instinctive but the product of reflection. No matter what stylistic disguise it assumes, it cannot escape the age on which it turns its back; restored, the language of the past becomes dialect, tingeing the language of the present. Archaizing is a symptom of nostalgia and if it pretends otherwise it degenerates into the self-conscious excesses of the Arts and Crafts movement at its worst.

Die Meistersinger makes no attempt to disguise its 'sentimentality' – it is only bad productions that have brought it into the realm of the arty-crafty. In terms of musical technique, this means that modern chromaticism, while reduced and kept in the background, is not expunged from the consciousness: the latent precondition of the style is *Tristan*, which is quoted at one point. The impression that diatonicism has been reinvested with its old, pre-chromatic rights is illusory: though unacknowledged and unexpressed, chromaticism is always present, and at certain moments it explicitly makes its presence felt. For instance, in the second subject of the overture – the E major cantilena which anticipates the Abgesang of the Prize Song – the chromaticism absent from the main melody is all the more prominent in the subordinate parts. What listeners have elsewhere to add for themselves is here 'composed out'.

The diatonicism of *Die Meistersinger* is somehow dreamlike, not quite real in the 1860s: not so much restoration as reconstruction. It is a 'second' diatonicism, in the sense that Hegel spoke of 'second' nature or 'second' immediacy, that is, something spontaneous that benefits from stores of awareness and reflection that have been accumulated previously. Nowhere, not even in *Parsifal*, is Wagner's music so artificial as in the appearance of simplicity with which it clothes itself in *Die Meistersinger*.

5

The archaizing tendency that colours the work as a whole also affects the musical forms. The formal types of earlier opera, rigorously banished from the *Ring* as concessions by drama to music, are much in evidence in *Die Meistersinger*. Large tracts are taken up with monologues, songs, ensembles, choruses and dances; each of the three acts concludes with a massed finale, just like a grand opera; and sometimes it appears as though the principle that dialogue forms the substance of musical drama (almost exactly as it does of spoken drama) is in abeyance, or, at the very least, threatened. While the text of *Die Meistersinger* comes the closest, among all the music dramas, to nineteenth-century realism, the style of its musical declamation is the furthest removed from realism. That does not mean, however, that Wagner had abandoned the idea of opera as drama and wanted to convert drama back into opera, but, on the contrary, that he was sure enough of the dramatic character of his music to trust it to convey the dramatic content even of apparently undramatic (even anti-dramatic) forms. Nobody would dream of denying that the impact of the third-act quintet is dramatic and not simply musical, in spite of the sudden suspension of the action while the dialogue gives place to five simultaneous soliloquies; there is no question of its being an interpolated concert piece.

On the other hand, it is important to recognize the artifice, the sentimental irony that attaches to Wagner's use of old forms. The predilection of his music in *Die Meistersinger* for the Bar-form of the historical mastersingers is a game.* Alfred Lorenz, the author of *Das Geheimnis der Form bei Richard Wagner*, and his adherents do less than justice to the unique formal character of *Die Meistersinger* when they

---

* A Bar is a strophic structure of two Stollen with the same musical setting for two stanzas of text, followed by an Abgesang which is metrically and musically different. It is more convenient to use the expression 'a Bar-form' in English, to avoid confusion with 'bar'.

discover Bar-form, the pattern A A B, as the central structural principle of all the music dramas, and do analytical violence to the musical fabric to demonstrate its omnipresence.

Walther's Trial Song ('Fanget an') in the final scene of the first act is an unusually extensive Bar-form of 160 bars. The two Stollen, musically the same, are in two parts, the first of which finishes with a regular, even emphatic perfect cadence and is also of a very different melodic character from the second ('In einer Dornenhecken'). One can therefore hardly blame Beckmesser – who is getting his just musical deserts – for failing to recognize Walther's Bar-form for what it is $(A^1 B^1 A^2 B^2 C)$ and interrupting him after the first part of the second Stollen (A^2), because he takes the one and a half Stollen $(A^1 B^1 A^2)$, with their unusual length, for an integrated ternary form. After a lengthy argument among the perturbed masters, Walther brings the Trial Song to a conclusion (beginning 'Aus finst'rer Dornenhecken') without being able to make any impression, dramatically, on the masters, who are by now all talking at once. (Musically, however, his cantilena soars triumphantly above the congested parlando of the ensemble: not even the most rigorous dramatist among opera composers could be expected to sacrifice his melody and allow it to stifle beneath a massed recitative for the sake of dramatic verisimilitude.)

The form is, then, ambiguous. A listener who does not know the music will do the same thing as Beckmesser, and take the beginning as a complete three-part form, a *da capo* aria. But this appearance of a return to a familiar operatic form is deceptive. When the Trial Song is resumed after the interruption, and concluded in spite of the continuing disturbance, the *da capo* form turns out to be merely a segment of a Bar-form: the second instalment $(B^2 C)$, unlike the first $(A^1 B^1 A^2)$, is not complete in itself, and to make formal sense of it the listener has to go back beyond the interruptions and relate it to the earlier part of the song. It is precisely in this interrupted form, creating the need for the listener to relate the second part to the first because it does not stand on its own, that the Trial Song provides a framework holding the scene, which is hundreds of bars long, together. Beckmesser's misapprehension of it, the dramatic motivation for the scene, also has structural significance for its form.

Wagner played comparable games even with insignificant formal details. It can hardly be accidental that Beckmesser's protest against a song which he does not recognize as being in Bar-form, because he is too impatient to wait for the end, is itself in Bar-form and even, unlike Walther's expansive cantilena, of normal song-length. Two motives, one distinguishing Walther as a knight in this bourgeois company and the other representing Beckmesser's envy,

come together to make an eight-bar period, which is then repeated with minor modifications, creating two consecutive Stollen. A third period, again beginning with the Knight motive, finishes differently, so that it can quite properly be called an Abgesang, which, according to the rules, should resemble the Stollen in some characteristics without being the same. But the use of Bar-form here is an exception, with the purpose of scoring a humorous point, and nothing could be more mistaken than to see in it a norm to which Wagner set himself to conform. The mistake that led Lorenz astray in his analyses lies in the equation of Bar-form with a procedure that derived from symphonic development technique: the construction of a 'model' from two or three motives, transposing it and finally hiving off details and working at them on their own account. To give the labels A A B to these three elements – the original model, the sequential repetition and the hiving-off – is to fail to recognize that song form and development form are mutually exclusive: in a nutshell, Bar-form is 'plastic', development form 'dynamic'.

The section following Beckmesser's protest ('Ein Wort, Herr Merker') illustrates what I mean. It appears at first, if one is in the toils of Lorenzian dogma, as though the Knight and Envy motives, in a different grouping, are forming another pair of Stollen (of nine and six bars); however, the motives are not just modified but substantially changed, and the continuation is nothing other than a transposition of the last three bars of the second of the apparent Stollen, and therefore does not qualify as an Abgesang. The passage is symphonic, an instance of motivic development, not a Bar.

6

The interlocking of the wilfully archaic and the modern, so that together they give *Die Meistersinger* its stylistic identity, is also characteristic of the leitmotivic technique (though it should be noted that the degree to which the expression is appropriate at all is doubtful). In a word, melody is restored, but not so much by way of reversion to earlier precedents as – paradoxically enough – hewn from the motives, the antithesis of melody. Reduced in the *Ring* and *Tristan* to the utmost brevity and pregnant significance, tending to musico-allegorical formulas, in *Die Meistersinger* motives combine to build up themes, or expand to create melodies, while it remains impossible to say with absolute certainty whether a motive is a fragment of a melody or, vice versa, a melody the development of a motive. The relationship remains equivocal.

The circumstance that the motives are not fixed formulas but mobile, interchangeable segments of themes and melodies is what makes it possible for a dense network of motivic relationships to link themes together within individual scenes. A paradigm of this process is provided by the 'baptism' scene in the third act, when the first version of Walther's Prize Song, which Sachs has written down, is given the name 'selige Morgentraumdeut-Weise' ('blessed morning-dream-interpretation song' – the name adds a strong whiff of mannerism to the 'old German' ambience). The various themes providing the musical basis of the passage – the Baptism chorale, the Mastersingers' theme, the Art motive, the chordal progression associated with Walther's dream, the Girl motive – seem at first hearing to retain their distinct individual identities, ranged side by side without any substantive connections having been forged between them. Such a juxtaposition would be perfectly legitimate in terms of musical form, if the themes grouped themselves together to make a plastic whole, whose parts and their relationships could be labelled according to an alphabetical scheme. But it is in fact difficult to discover an integrated formal shape in the way the themes are arranged, even one with fluid outlines. The musical coherence does not rest on the subordination of the themes to a formal scheme but on motivic links: the structure, to adopt a distinction made by Jacques Handschin, is not 'plastic' but 'logical'.

Distinctly individualized as the themes may appear to be, they are connected by common components and characteristics. The Art motive (b) is simply a fragment of the Mastersingers' theme (a) with a variant continuation. The rising tetrachord also recurs in the first line of the Baptism chorale (c), which moreover begins with a descending fourth like the Mastersingers' theme.

Both these elements, the descending fourth and the rising tetrachord, are found in the second line of the chorale (d), a variant of the first, in inversion. Finally in the Girl motive (e), though the fourth is expanded to a fifth, the tetrachord is retained. The only motive that does not similarly relate to all the others is the chordal progression, the musical emblem of the Morgentraumdeut-Weise itself.

The principle of the motivic linking is closely connected with that of the motivic working – the symphonic development technique: both are emanations of musical 'logic' as opposed to musical 'plasticity'. It is characteristic that the principle permits even a theme that would seem hostile and resistant to symphonic technique, the Baptism chorale, to be drawn into the motivic working. The scene begins ('Ein Kind ward hier geboren') with a statement of two lines of the chorale; then the first is repeated twice without the second, and finally the first bar alone is hived off and repeated; one cannot but be reminded of the symphonic development process of progressive hiving-off. Extremes are united without any suggestion of force. Art is inseparable from artifice: only the dilettante would wish to distinguish them. Such art is not only the subject of *Die Meistersinger* but also its outstanding feature.

Der Ring des Nibelungen

1

It is not known for certain whether Wagner read Friedrich Theodor Vischer's *Vorschlag zu einer Oper* (1844), recommending 'the Nibelung legend as the subject for a great heroic opera' ('zu einer großen heroischen Oper'), but it is likely enough that he did. (When he drafted *Siegfrieds Tod*, the first version of *Götterdämmerung*, in 1848 he classified it as 'eine große Heldenoper', which can only be translated by the same expression, 'a great heroic opera'.) The capacity to reach back into prehistory, into obscure mythological realms, is one of the basic attributes of music, as Vischer understood it, whereas complex processes of thought and reflection remain alien and inaccessible to music, which is a 'language of the emotions' with no command of concepts. Saga, with its simplicity of action and emotional spontaneity, in striking contrast to historical or modern subjects, seemed to Vischer foreordained for musical drama. Mythological heroes are men of few words, which makes them unequal to the rhetorical demands of spoken drama, but their taciturnity can be overcome in music (which Wagner called 'sounding silence'). In fact Vischer's *Proposal* contains a tacit historico-philosophical critique of music. Music is unable to express the 'true soul of our age', or can at best give only an approximate idea, because the 'more profoundly complex' is inaccessible to it; the world spirit has, to use Hegel's terminology, passed beyond the stage at which music was the natural medium for representing the essence and substance of the epoch.

Like Vischer, Wagner turned to the myth in search of the 'eternal fundamental emotions of the heart', of which he understood music to be the language. But what Vischer regarded as music's failing was for

Wagner its strength. In the historico-philosophical construction designed to bestow universal historical significance on the musical drama of the Nibelung's ring, the return to a mythological past simultaneously looked forward to a utopian future. The remote origins represented by the mythic action, reconstituted in music and made accessible by music to the emotional understanding of a different age, are also the goal towards which the history of mankind is travelling. The rule of law and coercion is to be replaced by the spirit of reconciliation and love, the language of thought and reflection by that of the emotions. To that extent mythic drama is the 'artwork of the future' that Wagner proclaimed it. Form and content converge: given presence and language by music, myth recoils from the complications and confusions of reflection and returns to the language of the emotions, and it thus becomes a form of expression that has its place in a future that is both desired and confidently expected; at the same time the myth provides the content, the dramatic idea of *Der Ring des Nibelungen*, which is about nothing less than the downfall of a world of law and force, and the dawn of a utopian age: though Siegfried and Brünnhilde fall victims to the old order, they are the first representatives of the new.

The music Vischer had in mind as the expression of the 'eternal fundamental emotions of the heart' was that of the opera of the eighteenth and early nineteenth centuries. Parcelled up in 'numbers', this music represented simple emotions one at a time, seldom 'mixed feelings', which were regarded with some distrust in operatic aesthetic theory. By contrast the music of the *Ring* could not be less simple or less single-minded. Over and all around the simplicity of the myth, and the vigour and sometimes violence of the stage action, there lies a musical commentary, a texture woven from many motives, the most outstanding characteristic of which is precisely that complexity of thought and reflection which, according to Vischer, was inaccessible to music. The spirit of Wagnerian music, from which myth is to be reborn as the 'artwork of the future', is itself affected by those reflective processes it purports to do away with. Wagner's aesthetic dogma was, of course, that art, if it was to be emphatically art and not merely artefact, had to make the impression of nature: every trace of the composer's working and intentions had to be expunged. His goal was aesthetic immediacy, but he was fully aware that that could be achieved only as 'second' immediacy: simplicity in art is the outcome of reflection in the studio, emotional effects the outcome of the composer's calculation, spontaneity the product of forethought, myth – the restoration of primeval origins in the 'artwork of the future' – the product of utopian aspirations.

'Second immediacy' is also the formula to describe what Wagner hoped for in the audience of the future (which would not be the same as the 'people' in the finale of *Die Meistersinger*, whose enthusiasm is tempered with crudity). If responses are to be governed by direct observation and emotion where thought and reflection ruled before, it is first necessary for reflection to have played its part effectively, so that it can then be forgotten. First-stage immediacy is nothing but blind emotion, wallowing in the music of the *Ring* as it flows past. The listener needs to be able to distinguish the musical motives, the 'emotional signposts along the drama's way', as Wagner called them, to recognize them when they recur, and to keep track of them as their relationships and functions change, if the music is not to roll on as the 'torrent' that the classicists among its denigrators have called it. It is only after reflection, and the suspension of reflection, that an emotion arises together with a power of musical observation that is more than aural gawping.

2

The *Ring* was over a quarter of a century in the writing, from 1848 to 1874; but the inconsistencies to be found throughout the work are less remarkable than the unity it preserves. It is easier, however, to sense the inner coherence than to define it in terms recognized in operatic and dramatic theory; the attempt to define it, to burrow down to the bedrock one vaguely senses is there, brings one up against the need to find some order in the strange confusion of all the elements – dramatic, epic and symphonic – that contribute substance to the work.

According to the rules laid down in classical tradition – and Wagner was not free of aspirations to classicism – dramatic form had to avoid epic traits. Aristotle wrote in the *Poetics*: 'The poet must take care not to give his tragedy an epic form. By epic I mean consisting of numerous stories, as if, for instance, someone were to try to dramatize the whole content of the *Iliad*.' The Nibelung myth, as Wagner sketched it early in October 1848, contains a very large number of stories. Finding that the material was distorted in the thirteenth-century *Nibelungenlied*, Wagner had gone back to the Edda in order to link the heroic tragedy of the death of Siegfried with the myths of the Germanic gods and so elevate the events to a cosmic drama. For the sake of this huge canvas he took the step that Friedrich Theodor Vischer, out of consideration for the dramatic rule of formal economy, had warned against:

> As narrated in the Edda an ancient curse is at work in the whole tragic course of events, the curse laid on the Nibelung hoard by the dwarf Andwari [the Alberich of Wagner's tetralogy]. . . But this is a connection that cannot be used in the opera; for accompanying the Edda back to those mythic beginnings is out of the question, if only because of the need for economy.

Wagner's prose sketch of October 1848 (*Die Nibelungensage* (*Mythus*), later published under the title *Der Nibelungen-Mythus Als Entwurf zu einem Drama*) includes the whole myth with all its narrative strands, from the theft of the gold to the deaths of Siegfried and Brünnhilde, an act of atonement which lifts the curse on the gold. The sketch distinguishes clearly between the prehistory and the action to be presented in the drama: everything up to the slaying of the dragon and the waking of Brünnhilde is prehistory, and the action begins with Hagen's plot and Siegfried's arrival among the Gibichungs. In the first version of his drama – written out in prose later in October and in verse in November 1848, with the title *Siegfrieds Tod*, later to be *Götterdämmerung* – this distinction serves to separate the myth of the gods from the heroic tragedy, what is recalled from what is enacted. From the standpoint of dramaturgical technique, *Siegfrieds Tod* is a failure: a gulf yawns between the prehistory and the action. Hagen's narration in the first act, telling the story of Siegfried and Brünnhilde, is the only epic passage which is integral to the drama, since it constitutes a part of the prehistory of the heroic tragedy which Hagen's plotting sets in motion. The other epic scenes, however, are clumsily imposed on the drama; the Norns' scene, Brünnhilde's encounter with the other Valkyries (corresponding to her scene with Waltraute alone in *Götterdämmerung*) and Hagen's dream expound the divine myth but are not integrated into the heroic tragedy. It is significant that these scenes are all absent from the original prose sketch; forced on him by narrative expediency, they do not belong to Wagner's original dramatic-cum-theatrical conception.

Wagner was forced to recognize that *Siegfrieds Tod* was not dramatically self-sufficient when he first attempted to set his text some two years after writing it, in the late summer of 1850. By this time he had fled from Dresden and was living in Zürich as a political exile. In June 1851 he wrote the text of *Der junge Siegfried* (later *Siegfried*) to amplify

Siegfrieds Tod; in a letter to Theodor Uhlig in November of the same year he mentioned his plan of enlarging the two-part drama to a tetralogy; the texts of *Das Rheingold* and *Die Walküre* were written in 1852. In the letter to Uhlig he wrote:

> Remember that – before I wrote the text of *Siegfrieds Tod* – I made a sketch which told the whole myth in its mighty context: in that first verse text I was making the attempt – such as I hoped would be feasible in our present-day theatre – to represent a major catastrophe from the myth while indicating that immense background. When I came to the complete musical realization and was at last obliged to think about theatrical practicalities, I recognized that what I had in mind was incomplete: the characters owe their immense, striking significance to the wider context, and that context was presented only to the mind, in the epic narratives. To make *Siegfrieds Tod* work, I therefore wrote *Der junge Siegfried*; but the very effect that had, of giving the whole far greater meaning, made it clear to me, as I dwelt on its scenic-cum-musical realization, that it was more than ever necessary to present the whole tale and its background in a directly perceptible form. I see now that to be perfectly understood in the theatre I must have the whole myth performed on the stage.

His argument that only what is seen and enacted on the stage will work in the theatre is based on his experience as an operatic composer; it would not apply to non-musical drama, where the epic narrative has a long-standing tradition. But even judged by the criteria of the non-musical theatre *Siegfrieds Tod* has one major failing: the divine myth is not properly linked to the heroic tragedy, the prehistory is not integrated into the action of the drama itself.

The dramaturgical difficulty that led Wagner to the hybrid decision to expand the tragedy of Siegfried into the tetralogy of the Nibelung's ring was closely bound up with a musical and compositional problem. Although – as his letters demonstrate – Wagner had plenty of musical ideas for it, *Siegfrieds Tod* proved impossible to compose. In 1850 he made composition sketches, which survive, for the Norns' scene, in which the myth of the gods is narrated in epic fragments – 'cosmic chitchat', as Thomas Mann put it. It was no accident that the sketch went no further: it was obviously beset with problems concerning not the musical declamation, the setting of the text, but the musical drama, the exposition of the central ideas of the mythic tragedy. The sketches lack musico-motivic substance. The mythic background, which, as Wagner said, gives the characters 'their immense, striking significance', remains musically colourless and thin, never rising above the level of mere melodic declamation. There is no question of the narratives in these sketches bringing the myth they recount to life, yet that was the function of music in drama, according to Wagner's aesthetic theory. (He wrote in *Opera and Drama* of 'realization for the feelings' – 'die Verwirklichung für das Gefühl' – that is, of making general or particular ideas and objects real in a manner that appeals directly to a region of perception where instinct and the emotions together recognize the truth contained in the evidence of the senses.) As an exposition of the divine myth the sketch of the Norns' scene fails musically.

The failure of the sketch is not isolated, however, but is closely related to the dramaturgical weakness of *Siegfrieds Tod* – the failure to integrate the narration of the myths into the action seen on the stage. Anything that had no foundation in the action was suspect to Wagner, who needed a textual and scenic *raison d'être* in order to shape a musical idea. (When he used the word 'motive' in his writings it did not refer to a melodic idea, but to its dramatic foundation or motivation.) In order to be understood beyond all shadow of doubt (and it was the ambition to be so understood himself that turned Wagner into an indefatigable exponent of his ideas) a musical idea – a 'melodic element' – had to be introduced in association with both words and an event on the stage, and it was the latter that was of crucial importance. The expression that stands out in the letter to Uhlig is 'scenic-cum-musical realization', which clearly means not so much that the stage realization is contained or prescribed in the text as that it only comes into being with the music, so that the events on the stage are connected with musical motives and the musical motives, vice versa, with events on the stage.

So the reason why the 1850 sketch of the Norns' scene fails is that Wagner needed to invent pregnant melodic motives imbued with dramatic significance for it – as the musical means of 'realizing' the narrated myths for recognition by the instinctive, non-verbal perceptions – but could not possibly do so in the absence of stage action 'bringing it to life'. In other words Wagner had not only dramaturgical but also musical reasons for writing first one and eventually three dramas to precede *Siegfrieds Tod*, to depict on the stage the events narrated in it:

it was essential if he was to create musical motives capable of 'realizing' the myth of the gods, the background to the heroic tragedy. It is only when a musical motive has been explicitly associated with something on the stage, with the gold, the ring, Valhalla or the restraints placed on Wotan's actions by his contracts and obligations (music cannot, of itself, express objects or concepts), that it can become a motive of reminiscence or a leitmotiv: a means, that is, of linking what is seen and spoken with what is not seen and not spoken.

The claim that events or objects seen on the stage establish the meaning of the important musical motives is open to the objection that Wagner ascribed to his motives not only the function of reminiscence but also that of presentiment ('Ahnung'), but that argument miscarries, for if a presentiment is never realized on the stage the musical motive that expressed it remains an unsolved cipher: an anticipation that is left unfulfilled. At the time when the myths of the theft of the gold, the building of Valhalla and Siegfried's fight with the dragon are narrated by the Norns in *Siegfrieds Tod*, they have not been seen on the stage, nor are being represented at that moment, and so Wagner could not give the words a 'motivic' setting but only a declamatory one.

It was the epic character of the Norns' scene that forced Wagner to abandon its composition in 1850. He seems, like Aristotle, to have blamed epic elements in drama in general for his difficulty. In a letter to Liszt of 20 November 1851 he wrote, apropos of expanding the two-part drama to four parts:

> The clarity of exposition that this will provide, by allowing everything that at present is narrated at such length either to drop out completely, or at least to be reduced to pithy allusions, will now give me plenty of room to intensify the abundance of associations to the most exciting degree, whereas with the earlier, semi-epic presentation I had laboriously to curtail and weaken everything.

But the presentation of the prehistory of Siegfried's tragedy on the stage, instead of merely in narrative, did not mean that the epic and reflective parts of the drama were reduced; far from shrinking they grew. In *Götterdämmerung* the Norns' scene is longer than it is in *Siegfried Tod*: the myths narrated in the latter have been made redundant by the stage action of *Das Rheingold*, and their place is taken by others, the even earlier tale of Wotan's damage to the World Ash, the consequent withering of the tree, and the foretelling of Valhalla's imminent destruction. Comparison of the Valkyries' scene in *Siegfrieds Tod* with Waltraute's scene in *Götterdämmerung*, or of the two versions of Hagen's dream, reveals a similar tendency to expand rather than to reduce epic sections.

Although on the face of it this contradicts what Wagner wrote to Liszt, it should cause no surprise. For the 'abundance of associations' that Wagner also wanted to create was inseparable from epic presentation. It is in the epic and reflective passages of *Götterdämmerung*, the narratives and the orchestral epic of the Funeral March, that the 'associative magic' unfurls which was praised so highly by Thomas Mann (that *Leitmotiviker* among novelists). Thus the epic element plays a paradoxical role in the *Ring*: if, as the 1850 sketches show, the epic exposition got in the way of a manner of composition that employed a motivic technique (and not merely musical declamation), on the other hand the epic recapitulation of what has already been shown visually actually creates opportunities for passages that are particularly rich in motivic development. The epic traits that Wagner the theorist wanted to banish from drama were restored out of musical necessity.

3

The myth Wagner narrated in the first prose draft of 1848, *Die Nibelungensage* (*Mythus*), stretches as far back as the mind can reach, yet it can also be interpreted as a political parable: it is an ambiguity that might remind someone with hypersensitive good taste of those constructions in Ancient Egyptian or Gothic style built in nineteenth-century ironwork. (Good Taste, however, has as little relevance to Wagner as to Mahler.)

The world is inhabited, in separate realms, by dwarfs (the Nibelungs), giants and gods.

> Out of the womb of night and death has sprung a race that dwells in Nibelheim (fog home), that is, in gloomy, subterranean fissures and caves. They are called Nibelungs; in spasmodic, restless activity they burrow their way (like worms in a corpse) through the bowels of the earth; they heat, refine and forge hard metals.

The unsavoury simile betrays that Wagner's sympathy for the industrial proletariat was mingled with an element of disgust.

Alberich has seized possession of the pure, noble gold of the Rhine, brought it out of the depths of the waters, and with great cunning forged from it a ring, which has given him supreme power over the whole of his race, the Nibelungs; in this way he has become their lord and master, compelled them to work for him alone thenceforth, and thus he has accumulated the immensurable Nibelung hoard, of which the most precious item is the Tarnhelm, which enables him to assume any shape and which he compelled his brother Reigin (Mime–Eugel) to make for him. So equipped, Alberich seeks dominion over the world and all that it contains.

The Nibelungs represent a threat to the giants and the gods alike. The giants build a castle – Valhalla – for the gods, as symbol and safeguard of the divine dominion, and ask for the Nibelung hoard in payment, because they fear Alberich.

By exercising their superior intelligence the gods succeed in capturing Alberich and demand that he ransom his life with the hoard; he tries to keep the ring alone; the gods – knowing well that the secret of Alberich's power lies in it – snatch the ring from him too; then he curses it: it shall be the destruction of all who possess it. Wotan hands the hoard over to the giants, but wants to keep the ring, so as to ensure his absolute dominion: the giants demand it and Wotan yields on the advice of the three fates (Norns), who warn him of the downfall of the gods themselves.

Instead of using the treasure and the power of the ring to increase their own might, the giants leave them 'on Gnita Heath, guarded by a giant dragon'. (Wagner calls the giants 'stupid'; but there is wisdom in their decision to have nothing to do with the ring and its curse, even if they have not consciously thought the matter out.) Wotan, heeding the warning of the Norns (Erda in the eventual version), decides to create support for his power among the human race. He recruits an army of dead heroes: the Valkyries 'lead those who have fallen in battle to Valhalla'. Only the ring ensures 'absolute dominion'; and Wotan's 'great idea' is that a hero, one not bound by the terms of the contract between the gods and the giants, shall kill the dragon and gain possession of the ring without being influenced by Wotan, who, as 'lord of contracts', may not incite the breaking of them. However, the independent hero whom Wotan needs does not acknowledge the laws of which Wotan is the representative (and whose runes are carved on his spear): the free man is lawless. (Wotan's contract with the giants, by a process of mythic analogy, stands for a world governed by contracts, agreements and laws that hold chaos and the rule of naked force at bay.) Siegmund, the chosen hero, son of Wälse–Wotan, commits adultery with Hunding's wife, Sieglinde, and marries her though she is his own sister. But if disregard of the law is on the one hand the essential condition whereby alone the free hero can fulfil Wotan's 'great idea', it is on the other hand the fateful circumstance that prevents its fulfilment; the element that promises salvation is, in a classic example of tragic irony, its own destruction. As the 'lord of contracts' Wotan is forced to punish adultery and incest. (In Wagner's view incest was not something unnatural, but illustrated nature in conflict with law. In *Opera and Drama* he wrote: 'Did Oedipus offend against human nature when he married his mother? Certainly not. Otherwise nature would have shown its offence by not permitting any children to be born to the marriage; but nature, if no other power, was quite content.') The sword Wotan had given Siegmund to arm him for the fight with the dragon is broken by Wotan's spear, the symbol of contracts and laws. The Valkyrie Brünnhilde, who tried to defend Siegmund against Wotan (her rebellion is obedience to Wotan's secret wish, though he is forbidden to wish it),

> is punished [by Wotan] for her disobedience: he expels her from the band of Valkyries and imprisons her on a pinnacle of rock where she, the virgin goddess, shall become the wife of the first man who finds her and wakes her from the sleep in which Wotan intends her to lie; she begs and obtains one favour, namely that Wotan will surround the rock with terrifying fire, so that she will be sure that only the bravest of heroes can win her.

'The bravest of heroes' is Siegfried, the son of Siegmund and Sieglinde. He grows up in the wilderness with Mime the Nibelung, the brother of Alberich. Under Mime's instruction he welds together the fragments of Siegmund's broken sword, and, incited by Mime, he kills the dragon guarding the Nibelung hoard.

> When he puts his finger, scalded by the dragon's blood, into his mouth to cool it, he involuntarily tastes the blood and thereby

is suddenly able to understand the language of the birds that are singing all around him in the forest. They praise Siegfried's prodigious deed, tell him about the Nibelung treasure in the dragon's cave, and warn him against Mime, who has only used him to get at the treasure and now intends to kill him, so as to have the gold for himself. On learning this, Siegfried kills Mime and takes the ring and the Tarnhelm from the hoard; he listens again to the birds, who advise him to win Brünnhilde, the most glorious of women. Siegfried now sets off, finds Brünnhilde's rocky stronghold, penetrates the fire burning round it, wakes Brünnhilde; joyfully she recognizes Siegfried, the most glorious hero of the Wälsung race, and yields herself to him: he weds her with Alberich's ring, which he places on her finger.

Siegfried, like Siegmund, has grown up outside the world of contracts and laws, in a wilderness Wotan avoids entering; the sword he bears is the counter-symbol to Wotan's spear. He is free, natural man, sought by Wagner in mythic prehistory, because he hoped for his coming in the future. Wagner was not troubled by the admission that the reverse face of 'instinct' is brutality (he saw himself as Wotan, the resigned and resigning god). But after fighting the dragon Siegfried makes his first contacts with the rest of the world and, precisely because he has had no previous knowledge of it, he gets into very deep trouble: the 'freest of heroes' becomes a puppet in a plot in which Hagen and Brünnhilde play the principal roles. The curse laid on the ring by Alberich lays Siegfried low through the agency of Hagen, Alberich's son. It is for Alberich that Hagen is supposed to win back the ring, the instrument and symbol of power. In Hagen's plot, the function of his half-brother and half-sister, the Gibichungs Gunther and Gudrun (Gutrune in *Götterdämmerung*), is to help in the deception, only to be deceived themselves.

Gunther learns from Hagen that Brünnhilde is the most desirable of all women and is aroused by him to wish to possess her, just when Siegfried arrives among the Gibichungs on the bank of the Rhine. Gudrun, thanks to the praise Hagen has lavished on Siegfried, falls in love with him, and, prompted by Hagen, welcomes him with a drink prepared by Hagen's magic art, with the power to make Siegfried forget that he ever knew

Brünnhilde or was married to her. Siegfried desires Gudrun as his wife: Gunther consents, on condition that he helps him win Brünnhilde. Siegfried agrees: they drink bloodbrotherhood and swear oaths in which Hagen takes no part.

The potion of oblivion is an embarrassment to Wagnerian exegetes of classical bent, whose taste is offended by so clumsily theatrical a prop. What they always fail to recognize is that the function of the potion is not so much to cause a particular effect as to clarify: in very much the same way as the love potion in *Tristan*, its purpose is to represent in theatrical, symbolic pantomime what is in fact the case, though it remains unspoken. Properly understood, it expresses and brings into play the tragic contradictions of Siegfried's situation, illustrating the dialectical ambivalence of his 'instinct'. In order to break the carapace of contracts and laws that at one and the same time upholds and confines Wotan's power, Siegfried must be the 'instinctive', unreflecting hero who obeys nothing but his own impulses. But though one face of this kind of self-reliance is liberty, another is limitation, confinement in the moment, in the here and now. Inasmuch as Siegfried, a 'pure fool' like Parsifal, belongs undividedly to the present, the past fades for him; lacking any faculty of memory, he falls victim to Hagen's plot. The cause of Siegfried's downfall lies in the tragic contradiction that his instinct and independence, which single him out to save himself and others from the entanglements of contracts and laws and the consequences of reflection, also invite disaster. The route that avoids catastrophe leads directly to it.

The rest of the action sees Hagen's plot run its course. Under cover of the Tarnhelm, which gives him the physical appearance of Gunther, Siegfried passes through the fire to Brünnhilde, robs her of the ring and takes her down to the boat where Gunther again takes his place.

With Brünnhilde obeying him in sombre silence, Gunther sails home along the Rhine: Siegfried, at Gudrun's side, and Hagen receive them as they arrive. Brünnhilde is horrified when she sees Siegfried as Gudrun's husband, and is amazed by his cool, friendly indifference to herself. When he points to Gunther as her husband she sees the ring on his finger, recognizes that some kind of deception has been practised on her and demands the ring, on the grounds that it does not belong to him, but was taken from her by Gunther: Siegfried refuses to give it to her.

It comes out that Siegfried deceived her in Gunther's shape, and Brünnhilde, Hagen and Gunther vow to kill Siegfried. The next morning, while hunting, Siegfried loses his way in a rocky gorge beside the Rhine. He meets the Rhinemaidens, who ask him to give back the ring, the gold stolen from the Rhine. But since they threaten him with disaster he refuses. The 1848 prose sketch goes on:

> Guiltless, he has taken the guilt of the gods upon himself, he atones for their wrong by his defiance, his independence.

Siegfried's 'defiance' – his fearlessness and self-reliance – is thus, like his 'instinct', simultaneously a means of salvation, something that beats a way out of the thicket of contracts and laws, and a means of destruction, which delivers him up to catastrophe. His 'folly' is both a shield and a snare.

Hagen kills Siegfried, but the murder, Alberich's revenge on Wotan, is in vain.

> Hagen goes to take the ring from the body, but it raises its hand threateningly; Hagen shrinks back in horror.

Brünnhilde, who sees through Hagen's plot in the end and recognizes Siegfried's innocence (insofar as the potion of oblivion exonerates him), immolates herself on his funeral pyre, in order to lift the curse and purge the ring, which returns to the Rhinemaidens, having been melted down again into the gold from which it was forged. The dominion symbolized by the ring, the dominion in which contracts and coercion were inseparable, is brought to an end and replaced by the 'realm of freedom' anticipated by Siegfried and Brünnhilde. In his *Origins of German Tragedy*, Walter Benjamin writes:

> The tragic sacrifice differs from every other in its victim – the hero – and it is both a first and a last. It is the last sacrifice offered up to appease the gods as the guardians of an old law; it is the first of a new kind of sacrifice where one dies for many, in a drama where human life and society assume new meanings.

4

'Such is the role of heroes in the whole history of the world: it is through them that a new world arises,' Hegel wrote in his *History of Philosophy*. There can be no denying that the conclusion of *Siegfrieds*

Tod, conceived in 1848, the year of revolution, was intended to be a mythic parable and dramatic anticipation of the dawn of a new world. 'Let the Nibelungs' servitude be ended, the ring shall enslave them no more.' But Brünnhilde's final words, addressed to Wotan, the god of the 'old law', are inconsistent with the general trend of the work, indeed they arguably contradict it altogether.

> Nur einer herrsche:
> Allvater! Herrlicher du!
> Freue dich des freiesten Helden!
> Siegfried führ' ich dir zu:
> biet' ihm minnlichen Gruß,
> dem Bürgen ewiger Macht!

> '*Let one alone rule: Allfather! Glorious! You! Rejoice in the freest of heroes! I bring Siegfried to you: render him loving welcome, for he is the surety of eternal power!*'

This ending might be defended with the argument that the deaths of Siegfried and Brünnhilde are sacrificial and atone for the guilt in which Wotan had steeped himself as 'lord of contracts'; the curse that was laid on the ring (or more accurately on power, of which the ring is the symbol) was a metaphor for the fatal paradox that the law, which is meant to uphold justice, operates by means of coercion and oppression; but that curse is now lifted by their deaths and a Utopia is about to be inaugurated where government will be free from guilt. Nonetheless, Brünnhilde's final words in the verse text directly contradict a passage in the 1848 prose sketch setting out a philosophical programme, which speaks beyond any shadow of misunderstanding of the gods' 'self-destruction'. In the language of Feuerbach, the world above humanity ('die Überwelt') is superseded when man recognizes himself in the god he has created for himself. Wagner wrote:

> It is for this high destiny of expiating their own [the gods'] guilt that the gods now educate mankind; their purpose will have been achieved when they have destroyed themselves in this human creation, namely when they have had to surrender their direct influence, faced with the freedom of the human consciousness.

(Ashton Ellis's attempt to explain away this passage as a later interpolation, so as to resolve the contradiction contained in the final lines of the verse text, is not borne out by the state of the manuscript.)

Insofar as the *Ring*, besides being a mythic tragedy, is also a political parable – Bernard Shaw interpreted it as the natural history of capitalism – it is perhaps appropriate to remember a political motive that influenced the dramatic conception and shaped the ending. A pamphlet Wagner published on 14 July 1848 with the title *What Relation do Republican Endeavours Bear to the Monarchy?* centres on a thesis that has obvious associations with Brünnhilde's final words: 'All that we can ask is that the king should be the first and most authentic of republicans. Is there anyone with a better calling to be the truest, loyalest republican than the prince himself?' The political paradox, the cloaking of a desire for conciliation in a dialectical disguise, turns up again in the drama: the monarch shall rule, but as a good republican.

But the political motive would hardly have had much effect on the drama without a structural correlative. The technical, dramaturgical element that gave it a foothold was a contradiction between the 'poetic intention' (to use Wagner's term from *Opera and Drama*) and its dramatic realization in a theatre. The fundamental idea of the work, as expressed in the prose sketch, is that the 'world of contracts', represented by Wotan, is to be replaced by a 'realm of freedom', as anticipated by Siegfried and Brünnhilde in one moment of rapture. But that idea is no more than a theory in *Siegfrieds Tod* – that is, before the drama was extended to a tetralogy: it is presented as a devout hope, but it is not realized in theatrical action. What would have been seen on the stage is Hagen's plot, to which Siegfried falls victim, and the disaster that attends the ring until the curse on it is lifted. But the myth and the gods remain 'unpresent', as Wagner put it; they are not 'brought to life'. Consequently the tragic dialectical argument outlined in the prose sketch is coarsened in the completed dramatic text and is nothing more than a simplistic contrast. It is not the Wotan–Siegfried antithesis that determines the action of *Siegfrieds Tod* but the black-and-white contrast of Hagen and Siegfried, as the frontmen for Alberich and Wotan. In terms of the dramatic structure, Wotan is Siegfried's god, as Alberich is Hagen's god, or anti-god; and therefore, when Hagen's plot fails and Siegfried saves by his death the idea that he had betrayed in life, dominion must fall to Wotan at the end. It may be false in terms of the conflict of issues, but that conclusion is the only proper one in terms of drama and the theatre, because what would have been seen on the stage is governed by simple contrasts. When Wagner extended his heroic tragedy, first to two dramas and finally to four, so as to expound the dialectical argument of Wotan's drama in visible stage action instead of merely outlining the idea of it, he had to alter the ending. *Siegfrieds Tod* became *Götterdämmerung*.

The fact that Wagner wrote no fewer than six versions of Brünnhilde's final lines is a sign of his uncertainty in the face of the divergence between the 'poetic intention' and the dramatic structure. Wagner the philosopher was at odds with Wagner the man of the theatre, for whom only what was seen on the stage could count. The first variant on the original version, which appears to date from as early as 1849, does not differ in its sense, though the praise of Wotan's lordship is toned down somewhat. It is only in the second that the rule of the gods is superseded by their downfall and 'blessed absolution in death'. Man, grown to full consciousness of himself, no longer needs the gods; he perceives – 'sees through' – them as the expression of, and the reason for, his inner and outer servitude.

> Machtlos scheidet
> die die Schuld nun meidet:
> Eurer Schuld entsproß der froheste Held,
> dessen freie Tat sie getilgt:
> erspart ist euch der bange Kampf
> um eure endende Macht:
> erbleichet in Wonne vor des Menschen Tat,
> vor dem Helden, den ihr gezeugt!
> Aus eurer bangen Furcht
> verkünd' ich euch selige Todeserlösung!

> '*Depart powerless, you who are now guilt-free; the most joyful hero was born from your guilt and expiated it by his free deed; you have been spared the terrified struggle for your waning power; grow pale in bliss before the deed of a human, before the hero whom you begot! Out of your dread I proclaim to you blessed absolution in death!*'

It is not certain when this second variant was written. It expresses in this dithyrambic manner what had already been briefly outlined in more philosophical language in the prose sketch of 1848, *Die Nibelungensage* (*Mythus*). However, if the work was to end convincingly with the downfall of the gods, that ending had to be justified dramatically, and not merely theoretically. For that, it needed to be preceded by the representation on the stage of Wotan's drama; that is, *Siegfrieds Tod* (the cast of which did not even include Wotan) needed to be supplemented by *Der junge Siegfried* (in whose final act Wotan's spear, the symbol of the 'old law', shatters on Siegfried's sword); this suggests that the variant may have been conceived in association with *Der junge Siegfried*, in the early summer of 1851.

The third variant dates from 1852, after the two-part drama had been extended to a tetralogy. (The fourth and fifth versions can be discussed only in association with an analysis of the score.) By this stage *Siegfrieds Tod* had turned into *Götterdämmerung*, which ends with Valhalla in flames.

> Denn der Götter Ende dämmert nun auf.
> So – werf' ich den Brand
> In Walhalls prangende Burg.
>
> '*For the day of the gods' destruction now dawns. Thus I hurl the brand at Valhalla's proud fortress.*'

The gods' 'blessed absolution in death', expressed only in words in the second variant, is made to happen on the stage in the third. The accentuation it gains from being seen is closely linked with the enlargement of the work into a tetralogy: the burning of Valhalla is not so much the end of *Siegfrieds Tod* (or of *Götterdämmerung*) as the end of the tragedy of Wotan, and it needs the emphasis of presentation on the stage in order to be effective over and above the compass of Siegfried's drama, as the end towards which all the earlier parts of the cycle have been directed.

The finale of *Götterdämmerung* also recalls Wagner's anarchist leanings and his association with Mikhail Bakunin, which was not as ephemeral as Wagner's own later testimony and the guardians of the Bayreuth tradition would have us believe. (Exactly as in the case of the original ending in the text of *Siegfrieds Tod*, the political and dramaturgical elements are inseparable and the political element becomes effective only when the dramatic structure provides a foothold for it.) On 22 October 1850 – eighteen months after fleeing from Dresden – Wagner wrote to Theodor Uhlig:

> But how shall we feel when Paris the monstrous is burned to the ground, when the fire spreads from city to city, when finally, wild with enthusiasm, they set light to these un-muck-out-able Augean Stables, in order to get some healthy air to breathe?

> After the fullest sober consideration, and with my feet firmly on the ground, I assure you that I no longer have faith in any revolution unless it begins with the destruction of Paris by fire.

The politics in this anarchist credo smack of literature, and the literature smacks of politics. The sage of Bayreuth was to revoke and disown it. In 1876, when Wagner invited the crowned heads of Europe to attend the first performance of *Götterdämmerung*, Karl Marx called him 'ein Staatsmusikant', someone who had sold his art to the establishment. He did not compromise the ending of *Götterdämmerung*, however, but let the reverse face of his view of monarchy stand, a Banquo's ghost from a lost revolution.

5

The expansion of the heroic legend to take in its mythic background, the growth of the drama of Siegfried into the tragedy of Wotan, was not only a matter of clarifying and realizing the 'poetic intention' of the 1848 prose sketch in theatrically effective terms, but also involved profound changes in the dramatic and theoretical conception of the work. One of the most important central motives of the *Ring* tetralogy of 1852, Alberich's renunciation of love, which gives him the power to forge the ring from the gold he steals, is absent from the 1848 prose sketch and from the text of *Siegfrieds Tod*. The subject of *Siegfrieds Tod*, which is still central to the *Ring* but is featured less prominently, is the process whereby the 'world of contracts' gives way to the 'realm of freedom', and god-made laws to human 'instinct'. The old law engraved in runes on Wotan's spear is inseparable from guilt: force in the service of good, even though it may appear justified by its end, is still force.

> The purpose of their [the gods'] higher world order is moral consciousness: but they are tainted by the very injustice they hunt down; from the depths of Nibelheim the consciousness of their guilt echoes back threateningly.

Then in *Opera and Drama* (1850–1) Wagner outlined a political argument that is nothing other than Wotan's dialectical predicament.

> Since political states were first set up, there has been no step in history which, however strong may have been the determination to strengthen the state when it was taken, has not led

towards its downfall...the necessity of free self-determination
of the individual, which is common to all organs of society,
amounts to the destruction of the state.

(Like Marx, Wagner supposed that the state would wither away when
its citizens ceased to be 'alienated'.) Re-expressed in the metaphor of
his drama, the building of Valhalla, which was undertaken with the
intention of providing a stronger basis for Wotan's rule, has to be paid
for with the ring stolen from the Nibelung, and so is the very means of
attracting the disaster that attends the ring.

On the other hand, freedom from the gods' laws is equally liable to
inculpate the free man (in the drama, Siegfried is the physical embodiment of such freedom and possession of the ring destroys him).
Siegfried's 'freest deed' is to kill Fafner, the dragon who guards his
'property', the Nibelung hoard ('property is theft'): but that killing
is murder all the same. Moreover Siegfried's freedom is still virtually
unconscious; he is completely absorbed in the immediate present, and
while, on the one hand, this liberates him from-the past with its laws
and legacy of coercion and so enables him to perform the 'freest deed',
on the other hand, as explained above, it is also the reason why he falls
into the tragic trap laid for him. It is only in Brünnhilde that freedom
grows to self-awareness: she was divine and has become human, that is,
the gods' 'self-destruction' and their superseding by the 'freedom of
the human consciousness' have actually taken place in her; it is through
her that 'the new world dawns'.

While in *Siegfrieds Tod* the tragedy of the events – of the myths in
the role of political parables – has a conceptual foundation in the
dialectical maze of law, freedom and coercion, the mainspring of the
action of the *Ring* is the renunciation and cursing of love for the sake
of power. Alberich, the lord of the underworld, curses love in the first
scene of *Das Rheingold* with crude plebeian explicitness; with Wotan,
'Light-Alberich', the renunciation is less drastic, more the striking of
an aristocratic attitude:

> Als junger Liebe
> Lust mir verblich,
> verlangte nach Macht mein Mut.

> '*When the delights of young love faded for me, I longed in my heart
> for power.*'

To satisfy Wagner, his drama had to unite dialectical argument and theatrical effectiveness, and so he had to seek a tragic dialectic that would be more than a simple contrast of black and white: such a contrast still seems platitudinous even when, instead of being merely a confrontation between characters (Alberich and Hagen versus Siegfried and Brünnhilde), it is developed inside the one character (Wotan). If the dramatic dialectic was to be truly tragic, on the one hand the 'simple' contrasts needed to be more subtly differentiated, and on the other the argument needed to be of such a quality as to span the entire tetralogy, composed as it is from so much heterogeneous material. An interpretation of the *Ring*, if it is to do justice to Wagner's artistic intelligence, must explain the thematic and conceptual unity of the action, whether Wotan or Siegfried holds the centre of the stage. (The thesis that Siegfried's drama is only a corollary of Wotan's tragedy may appear illuminating at first, but comes to grief on the theatrical fact that Siegfried's drama occupies the tetralogy's two longest parts.)

The idea that enabled the dramatic motive of the renunciation of love – absent altogether from *Siegfrieds Tod* – to be tragically creative was Wagner's recognition of lovelessness as fear. In a letter to August Röckel of 25 January 1854, he explained some changes he had made in the text of *Das Rheingold*.

> Instead of the words 'ein düstrer Tag dämmert den Göttern: in Schmach doch endet dein edles Geschlecht, läßt du den Reif nicht los!' ['a dark day dawns for the gods: your noble race shall end in shame, if you do not surrender the ring!'] I now have Erda say 'Alles was ist – endet: ein düstrer Tag dämmert den Göttern: Dir rat' ich, meide den Ring!' ['All things that are, perish: a dark day dawns for the gods: I warn you, yield up the ring!'] We must learn to die, and die in the most complete sense of the word; fear of the end is the source of all lovelessness, and it grows only where love itself is already fading.

Both fear and fearlessness – Wotan's fear and Siegfried's fearlessness – are elements of the tragic argument of the *Ring*. And because these antithetical elements are drawn inexorably into the same tragic situation, they link Wotan's drama with Siegfried's, the divine myth with the heroic tragedy.

In warning Wotan of the gods' downfall in the closing scene of *Das Rheingold*, Erda acts like the oracle in classical tragedy, whose prophecy is a snare: the warning is a prophecy which is fulfilled because it was spoken. It is the very ways by which the person marked by destiny attempts to escape his fate that lead him, by a tragic irony, to disaster; what should have saved him destroys him. The 'great idea' by which Wotan thinks he will safeguard Valhalla, the idea that a hero 'free of the gods' laws' shall kill the dragon whom Wotan himself may not slay, proves disastrous: by killing Fafner Siegfried rouses the dormant curse. (In the 1848 prose sketch the Norns – instead of Erda – warn the gods of their impending fate, but the oracle is not fulfilled; this is a dramatic weakness and an argument against the legitimacy of the original ending: fearful expectation of a doom foretold by omens creates a tension which can be released in a good outcome only in comedy, not in tragedy.)

Just how important the motive of fear and fearlessness was for Wagner is illustrated by a letter to Theodor Uhlig of 10 May 1851, about the decision to write a 'Young Siegfried':

> Haven't I written to you once before about a subject for a comedy? It was the folk story about the boy who leaves home 'to learn fear' and is too stupid ever to learn it. Imagine the shock I had when I suddenly realized that that boy is none other than: young Siegfried, who wins the treasure and wakes Brünnhilde!

But the fearlessness which enables Siegfried to fulfil Wotan's 'great idea' is also the agency of his destruction. When the Rhinemaidens ask Siegfried to give them the ring, and threaten him with disaster, his fearlessness makes him disdain the warning.

> Denn Leben und Leib
> – sollt' ohne Lieb'
> in der Furcht Bande
> bang ich sie fesseln –
> Leben und Leib –
> seht! – so
> werf' ich sie weit von mir!

> *'For life and limb – if, terrified, I am meant to chain them in the bonds of fear, without love – see! thus I throw them away!'*

(This is accompanied by a stage direction requiring Siegfried to pick up a clod of earth and toss it over his shoulder.) This statement, made rather cryptic by Wagner's decision to omit the four lines beginning 'sollt' ohne

Lieb" from the full score, only reveals its meaning if we recognize the equation of love and fearlessness (and of lovelessness and fear) as a fundamental dramatic motive in all Wagner's work. If fear is the death of love, on the other hand the physical death that has no terrors for Siegfried is the salvation of the love that he has unknowingly betrayed.

6

In 1854 Wagner read Schopenhauer's *The World as Will and Idea* at the prompting of Georg Herwegh. The philosophy of renunciation, of 'denial of the will', seemed to match his own sense of being quite without consolation – recognition of which is its own consolation. He wrote to August Röckel in February 1855:

> Although he [Schopenhauer] has set me off in a direction that diverges somewhat from my previous one, the change was only in accordance with my own feelings about the essential nature of the world, which cause me deep suffering.

It was no fluke that Schopenhauer's philosophy should have struck Wagner with such force at the very time when he was composing *Die Walküre*. His convictions were always inclined to develop out of his works, rather than vice versa, and it is in the second act of this work that Wotan resigns himself and gives up his plans as hopeless, recognizing the impasse where he is trapped. That Siegmund stands outside the law is the condition enabling him to commit the 'freest deed', as Wotan intended, but it also means that Wotan, as 'lord of contracts', must take action against him.

> Auf geb' ich mein Werk;
> eines nur will ich noch:
> das Ende – –
> das Ende! –
> Und für das Ende
> sorgt Alberich!
>
> '*I give up my work; I wish for only one thing more: the end, the end! And Alberich will take care of the end!*'

Wagnerian hermeneutists of a philosophical bent, under whose gaze dramatic texts transform themselves into allegories, have not hesitated to interpet Wotan as an embodiment of the 'will', the resignation to which he gives way as the 'denial of the will', and the tetralogy as a whole as an illustration of Schopenhauer's metaphysics in words and music. Wagner himself believed that Schopenhauer had enabled him to understand his work for the first time, as he wrote to August Röckel on 23 August 1856:

> I was hardly aware of how in the execution – in fact, essentially even in the planning – of my work I was unconsciously following a quite different, much deeper view of things [i.e. the Schopenhauerian]. Unwittingly, instead of one phase in the evolution of the world, I was seeing the very essence of the world, in every imaginable phase, and recognizing its nothingness. The result, of course, as I remained loyal to my view of things and not to my concepts, was that something quite different came into being from what I had actually planned. Yet I recall eventually forcing my intention on the work – just the once – in the tendentious closing lines Brünnhilde addresses to the bystanders, decrying possessions as reprehensible and praising love as the only source of happiness, without (unfortunately!) having really come to terms with that same 'love', which we have observed, as the myth has run its course, creating some pretty thorough havoc!

Wagner was referring to the lines with which he ended the version of 1852–3, which he left out when he finally came to compose *Götterdämmerung* (though he did set them on their own as a present for King Ludwig).

> Nicht Gut, nicht Gold,
> noch göttliche Pracht;
> nicht Haus, nicht Hof,
> noch herrischer Prunk;
> nicht trüber Verträge
> trügender Bund,
> nicht heuchelnder Sitte
> hartes Gesetz:
> selig in Lust und Leid
> läßt – die Liebe nur sein.

> *'Not goods, not gold, nor godly splendour; not house, not land, nor lordly pomp; not the cheating covenant of cheerless contracts, not the harsh laws of lying custom: rapture in pleasure and pain comes – from love alone.'*

In other words, Wagner exchanged the philosophy of history for an existential philosophy, and rejected utopianism in favour of resignation. The *Ring* does not portray 'one phase in the evolution of the world' – the transition from a 'world of contracts', where law and coercion unite in an unhappy alliance, to a 'realm of freedom', anticipated in the original state of the love of Siegfried and Brünnhilde, before the tragic confusion; it portrays the 'very essence of the world', in which it is impossible to interfere, hoping for change, without the will for something better necessarily introducing something worse. Schopenhauer condemned optimism as 'wicked', and it was in that spirit that Wagner demolished and denied the utopianism of the *Ring*. The love of Siegfried and Brünnhilde is represented as bringing 'havoc' in its wake, a blind, destructive 'will' in a world of anguish and confusion. Expressed as a paradox, the 'essence of the world' consists of the tragic contradiction that the 'essence', love, cannot become reality but rather destroys itself in the very effort to become reality and establish itself in reality. Viewed in this light, the deaths of Siegfried and Brünnhilde, too, are not the last sacrifices to the old law, in order that a Hegelian 'new world may dawn', but set the seal on the futility that defeats every attempt to make the essence into the reality. The only thing left is resignation, and the tragic hero of the *Ring* is not Siegfried but Wotan.

Wagner's own Schopenhauerian interpretation of the *Ring* has hardly ever been challenged, since it suits the image of him as the revolutionary who recanted – an image shared by his adherents and his opponents alike. (The former speak of the triumph of good sense, and the latter of betrayal, but that does not affect the common premiss.) Yet it does not hold water. It is true that Wotan is a figure of resignation in *Die Walküre*, and a 'wanderer' in *Siegfried*, roaming about like his own ghost. But the 'end' that he 'wills' is not the end of the world, but the downfall of the gods; he is weary to death of the old system of rule and the guilt in which it has entangled itself. In the words of the 1848 prose sketch, his resignation is the gods' 'self-destruction', whereby the way is opened for mankind to attain to consciousness of its freedom. And even though Wotan fears an end brought about by Alberich, he nonetheless hopes for a cessation of the gods' rule in a way which will release mankind from coercion and fear. At the end the ring, the symbol of force and oppression, is melted back into the Rhine's gold from which it was forged. It is thus – and not as the 'denial of the will' – that the gods' 'absolution in death' is 'blessed'.

Wagner's reference to the 'havoc' wrought by love – and when he put 'love' in quotation marks it was a crude offence against his own work – is also wide of the mark. It is not because of the nature of their love in itself that Siegfried and Brünnhilde get embroiled in a tragic misunderstanding: it does *not* destroy itself in the very effort to become reality and establish itself in reality; it is destroyed by an outside agency and falls victim to a world in opposition to it. Most important of all, their love was a reality before they were tricked and misled, and the fact that it was is a promise for the future.

The letter to Röckel cannot be reconciled with the work itself, and Wagner eventually revoked the Schopenhauerian interpretation himself, though only by implication and in one of his less public utterances. On the one hand there is the significance of his breaking off the composition of *Siegfried* at the end of the second act in the summer of 1857: in the frame of mind expressed in the letter to Röckel he could not have composed Brünnhilde's awakening in the third act. But in a letter he wrote to Mathilde Wesendonk eighteen months later, on 1 December 1858, he spoke of 'broadening' and partly 'correcting' Schopenhauer's philosophy. The 'correction' amounts to nothing less than a complete reversal of it:

> Namely, I want to demonstrate that there is a saving way that leads to the complete pacification of the will through love, which no philosopher, especially not Schopenhauer, has ever recognized; it's not an abstract love of mankind, but real love, the love that blossoms from sexual love, that is, from the attraction between man and woman.

The Utopia of love as absolution from fear – the Utopia realized in Siegfried and Brünnhilde – was restored, even though flying a Schopenhauerian flag. And with that Wagner was able to set the love story of Siegfried and Brünnhilde to music.

7

The text of the *Ring* owes its characteristic form to Stabreim, the alliterative verse which has been praised and vilified in equal measure, and which Wagner made the effort to justify by a dialectical interpretation of the history of poetry and music in *Opera and Drama*. His adoption of the ancient German verse form was not merely in the interests of atmosphere, an attempt to assimilate the diction to the subject of the drama; like the myth expressed in it, the Stabreim was intended as a means of restoring the 'purely human' to the text (which, as the 'artwork of the future', looked forward to the time when 'alienation' would be driven out by reality). Writing his alliterative 'staves', Wagner felt close to the shattered primeval origins of poetry.

In spite of Wagner's theory it must be said that musically, as the precondition and foundation of the composition, the alliteration is of little moment. But the Stabreim has a secondary characteristic which is important, though negative, and that is its complete lack of metrical regularity. Wagner's lines of Strabeim differ from his old German models in that the number of strong accents is irregular: some lines have two, others three or even four. The consequence is nothing less than the dissolution of musical periodic structure, the syntax that had provided the framework of both instrumental and vocal melodic writing for the past hundred years and more. Rhythmic regularity – schematism, if you want a pejorative term – contributes to musical structure, in association with harmony and motivic material. Melodic elements of the same length tend to complement each other and, if the harmony and motivic material assist, or at least do not actively prevent it, combine to make a group. The quantitative element performs a qualitative, syntactic function. In its classical form, musical syntax is hierarchic: two bars combine to form a phrase, two phrases a half-clause, two half-clauses – antecedent and consequent – a period. A four-bar group may shrink to three bars or extend to five without affecting the principle; but if the syntax is to remain within the listener's grasp, it is a precondition of the exception, the departure from the regular norm, that the rule should have impressed itself firmly on his or her musical consciousness.

In Wagner's musical syntax the classical norm has been suspended. The lines of Stabreim at the beginning of Waltraute's narration in the first act of *Götterdämmerung* are singly and collectively irregular; it is as though Wagner regarded the alliteration as justification and compensation for the rhythmic irregularity. This would mean that, slight though its manifest musical significance is, the Stabreim is the poetic cause and justification of Wagner's decision to dispense with musical periodic regularity and, in consequence, with a regular pattern of strong accents.

1 Seit er von dir geschieden,
2 zur Schlacht nicht mehr
3 schickte uns Wotan;
4 irr und ratlos

5 ritten wir ängstlich zu Heer.
6 Walhalls mutige Helden
7 mied Walvater:
8 einsam zu Roß
9 ohne Ruh' und Rast
10 durchstreift' er als Wandrer die Welt.

Only an over-zealous apologist would claim that the alliteration is a means of stressing semantic associations by the sound of the words, that is, that the alliterative syllables coincide with the accents in the meaning. Quite often a principal accent ('dir' in l. 1, 'einsam' in l. 8) is not the rhymed syllable ('schied', 'Roß'), or the rhyme links an accented word ('mied' in l. 7) with an unimportant one (the adjective 'mutige' instead of the noun 'Helden' in l. 6). If therefore the alliteration plays little part in associating words – and one could hardly expect anything else – the dissociative effect of the irregularity of the metre is all the clearer. The melodic phrases corresponding to the lines of the text in this passage vary in length according to no apparent rule: $1 + \frac{1}{2} + 1 + 1 + 1 + 2 + 1\frac{1}{2} + 1 + 1 + 1\frac{1}{2}$ bars. It is no overstatement to call it musical prose. Even the groups of lines created by semantic association, that is, lines 1–3, 4–5, 6–7 and 8–10, are irregular in the number of bars they take up: $2\frac{1}{2}$, 2, $3\frac{1}{2}$ and $3\frac{1}{2}$ respectively. The gaps occurring where vocal phrases begin or end with half-bars are filled with orchestral motives, but even the musical syntax resulting from the interlocking of vocal and instrumental melodies is anything but regular. First of all, groups of two, three and four bars alternate with each other in the 'orchestral melody', as Wagner called it (and the four-bar group at the end of the passage under consideration, the motive of Wotan's restless wandering, is made up, not of $2 + 2$ bars, but of $1 + 2 + 1$ bars). Secondly, vocal phrases and instrumental motives not infrequently overrun each other, instead of being synchronized: the first vocal phrase, $2\frac{1}{2}$ bars long, is expanded by the orchestra to make a three-bar group, but the third bar, the last so far as the vocal phrase is concerned, functions in the orchestral melody as the first bar in a two-bar phrase. Thirdly, the orchestral motives in the *Ring* are more accurately described as successive than as harmonically and melodically complementary, or as antecedent and consequent clauses of periods in the manner of classical musical syntax. Wagner's basic syntactical form is paratactic, not hypotactic.

Periodic structure – in ruins for long stretches of the *Ring* – had been the foundation of all musical form since the 1720s. In the Classical period, the decisive structural element, the source of the coherence and integration in any musical work, was not the thematic material and its development, but the syntax, the grouping of the constituent parts. (This was true above all of vocal music, whose aesthetic pre-eminence was hardly doubted even in the early nineteenth century, Beethoven not-withstanding.) Musical form was the outcome of the grouping and linking together of periods, mutually distinguished and related by their various functions: introduction, theme, development section, concluding section or coda; more obvious functional differentiation simultaneously signified closer formal integration. In all Wagner's earlier works, up to and including *Lohengrin* – that is, in the operas which it is wrong to classify as music dramas (to do so suppresses the inner history of Wagner's oeuvre for the sake of the unity of the Bayreuth tradition) – the musical form is determined primarily by the syntax. Periodic structure in them is regular or even schematic: groups four and eight bars long succeed each other without any disruption of the syntactic structure to upset the listener's sense of a reliable regularity, which, however unobtrusive, is of decisive importance for the cantabile impression it all makes.

It was not until the *Ring* – at least in large sections of it, and more consistently in *Götterdämmerung* than in *Rheingold* – that Wagner disrupted or annulled the rules of classical syntax. The correlative of the musical prose resulting from the discarding of periodic structure was leitmotivic technique, or, to be more precise, the extension of the technique to the entire work. From *Rheingold* onwards, the basis of Wagner's musical form is no longer primarily syntactic but motivic. The complex of motivic association that spreads over the entire tetralogy in a dense network has to assume the form-building role previously performed by regular syntax, with its articulation in periods whose functional differentiation was the guarantee of their formal integration: motivic association has to replace regular syntax or justify and compensate for its decline.

The argument as to whether leitmotivic technique can be traced back to Weber, Grétry or even Monteverdi is as great a waste of time as the controversy as to whether the decisive stage in Wagner's case is represented by *Die Feen*, *Der fliegende Holländer* or the *Ring*. What is important is the recognition that the compositional innovation of the *Ring*, the process of spreading a dense web of leitmotive over the whole work so that they are almost omnipresent, was a qualitative leap in the history of leitmotivic technique. In *Lohengrin* the leitmotive, though sometimes prominent and dramatically significant, are compositionally peripheral: they are interpolations in the periodic structure that provides the musical framework. It was only in the *Ring* that they became essential structural factors. In 1850–1, at the time when he was trying to become clear in his mind about how to compose the drama he had started to write, Wagner wrote in *Opera and Drama:*

> The principal motives of the dramatic action, having become distinct melodic elements that perfectly realize their content

– he conceived of the music, the leitmotive, which he called 'melodic elements', as the 'realization of the poetic intention' for the listeners' instinctive perceptions –

> shape themselves, as they recur in their manifold relationships, their purpose and meaning always clear (resembling rhyme in that), into a unified artistic form

– in other words, the musical complex of motivic associations plays an essential role –

> which spreads not merely over limited areas of the drama, but over the whole drama, linking it all together.

It appears from that that the linking of the 'melodic elements' – the musical 'signposts for the emotions', as he also called them in a drastic metaphor – is founded in the 'poetic intention' and not in abstract principles of musical form. On the other hand the 'unified artistic form', with its musical foundation, which 'spreads over the whole drama', takes the place of the closed dramatic form, which it was still Wagner's intention to give *Siegfrieds Tod*, but which fell apart in the epic sprawl of different plots resulting from the expansion of the drama of Siegfried to the tetralogy of the Nibelung's ring. Motivic technique, the process of spinning a web of metaphors, whether poetic or musical, over a work, is characteristic of open or epic forms of drama (think of Büchner and Maeterlinck). That it was possible to bring – or force – together in the *Ring* such a motley array of subjects as the myth of the gods, the drama of the Wälsungs, the fairy tale of young Siegfried setting out to learn fear, and the tragedy of Siegfried and Brünnhilde, without gaps and rifts being everywhere apparent, is due to the leitmotivic technique, the magic power of metaphor and allegory to draw the listener into a world of musico-poetic relationships where, in the end, everything seems to belong with everything else.

To try to decide which of the elements that distinguish music drama from opera are primary or fundamental, and which secondary – the mythic subject matter, the open dramatic form, the irregular verse rhythm, the dissolution of musical periodic structure, or the extension of leitmotivic technique over the whole work – is not just impossible, it is unnecessary. It is enough to recognize their interrelationship and to be aware of the problems that had to be solved before it could be satisfactorily established: that the residue of those problems is virtually imperceptible in the finished work is one of the clearest proofs of its artistic rank.

Das Rheingold

1

The conclusion of *Das Rheingold*, the entry of the gods into the fortress Valhalla, is not as triumphant as the music, the Rainbow Bridge motive, allows a listener to believe if its brilliance hides from him the true nature of what has just happened. In the depths the betrayed Rhinemaidens are lamenting the theft of the gold, while the gods laugh at them:

> Falsch und feig
> ist, was dort oben sich freut!

> *'False and faint-hearted is what revels above!'*

Fafner, one of the giants who built the fortress, has killed the other, Fasolt: the first victim of the curse on Alberich's ring. And Wotan's theft of the ring, at Loge's suggestion, to pay for the building, was an act of brute force. 'From the depths of Nibelheim the consciousness of their [the gods'] guilt echoes back threateningly.' Dismayed by Erda's warning of the gods' doom, appalled by Fafner's murder of Fasolt, Wotan starts to think about how to lift the curse on the ring. He is not permitted to own the ring himself; but the 'great idea' he now conceives, of a hero who shall gain possession of it, is self-deception. Only Loge, the god of fire, but more an elemental spirit than a god, is unaffected and therefore aware of the illusion the gods are labouring under.

> Ihrem Ende eilen sie zu,
> die so stark im Bestehen sich wähnen.

> *'They are hastening towards their end, believing themselves secure.'*

(Loge's paradoxical role in *Das Rheingold*, combining the apparently irreconcilable functions of the tenor, musically, and the *raisonneur*, dramatically, provokes one to parody Schopenhauerian interpretations of the *Ring*: if Wotan represents the 'will', Loge embodies the 'intellect', the instrumental faculty of reason, which obeys the will but in the end, realizing the blindness of the will, dissociates itself from it and returns to a disembodied state, which signifies absolution.)

How did Wagner compose this ending? Was he looking through Loge's baleful eyes, or was he dazzled like the gods? The Rainbow Bridge motive consists of nothing more than a broken chord of G♭ major, extended over an entire period: a flickering but stationary sound, whose movement is all within itself. But whereas at the beginning of the work, in the E♭ major of the prelude, the simplicity was an allegory of the elemental universe and an image in sound of the primeval origin of things, at the end, after the music has been through so much development and elaboration, it creates the impression of reduction and of a simplification which is not to be trusted. It does not express certainty and firmness so much as self-deception about the disaster and confusion that lie behind the current state of affairs and will not be made to disappear by being ignored. The stationary sound that represents nature at the beginning is, at the end, 'second' nature, intended to draw a consoling veil over the story and its entanglements, but subject to the listener's reservations.

The first statement of the Sword motive, symbolizing Wotan's 'great idea' in the final scene, is equally ambiguous. The motive, another broken triad, is stated in a key, C major, that obtrudes as an interpolation in the tonal context. The key was therefore introduced for the sake of the motive, and if its significance is to be understood, time will be well spent sketching the 'prehistory' of C major in *Das Rheingold*.

It is in C major, a key that traditionally expresses simplicity and integrity, that the motive of the gold is stated in the first scene. The motive and the key recur together at the end of Loge's narration in the second scene, but the fact of being quoted transforms them, so that they are as deceptive as Loge's speech, which lies as it tells the truth: Loge appropriates the Rhinemaidens' plea for Wotan to return the gold to the water (which would bring the tragedy to a rapid and utopian ending), because he knows Wotan is too deluded to do so; he gives this piece of good advice fully intending it to be ignored and secure in the knowledge that it will be. Wagner, armed with the ability to give tonal relationships expressive and allegorical significance, matched this moral shiftiness with a purely musical correlative, which can be defined in precise technical language. The C major in Loge's narration is not, as it is in the first scene, self-sufficient and self-justifying but appears in the role of a subordinate or auxiliary of B minor, and this relationship to B minor determines or colours its character. At first the C major is introduced unobtrusively, lasting for one bar in a subordinate (neapolitan) relationship to B minor ('Nur einen sah ich'); then it is heard during the course of an antecedent clause ('Des Rheines klare Töchter klagten mir ihre Not'); and finally it provides the tonal basis for the quotation of the Gold motive, in what appears at first to be a complete, tonally self-sufficient period ('das Gold dem Wasser wiedergebest'), but goes on to cadence into B minor. So the relationship of the C major to the B minor is always that of the lowered supertonic. This lowering is nothing but chromatic variation, a colouring and darkening of the interval: C major, in its normal character the expression of clarity and integrity, thus occurs in the tonal context of B minor as the result of chromaticization. The tonal ambiguity exactly expresses Wagner's 'poetic intention': simplicity enters a twilight area where truth and deception are impossible to distinguish.

The same tonal relationship is used again for an expressive or allegorical purpose in the fourth scene. The Curse motive, the musical metaphor for Alberich's curse on the ring, is stated in B minor, and once more C major appears in the neapolitan relationship. The Gold motive in C major (sometimes modified to C minor) is juxtaposed with a motive in B minor that symbolizes Alberich's dominion over the Nibelungs (F♯-D-E-F♯). B minor is the background from which C major emerges with deceptive clarity, in an orchestral passage representing Wotan's contemplation of the ring he has just seized, oblivious to all else in a dream of eternal dominion. The key, C major, is on as uncertain a foundation as the situation it expresses and – in more senses that one – betrays.

At the end of the work the Sword motive (representing the 'great idea') appears, in the key of C major, in the context of A♭ major and D♭ major, and not as the direct result of chromaticization and darkening. Nevertheless a residue of twilight ambiguity clings to it, as long as the listener's musical memory does not fail him; for the character of a key, in very much the same way as a motive, cannot be dissociated from its past history. Thus Wagner's 'poetic intention' was twofold: a C major that stood for integrity, the symbol of the 'freest deed' of a hero who would destroy the 'dreary contracts' of the god-made law; and a C major that, for all its apparent solidity, we know to be hollow. In the aesthetics of Wagner's works – which should not be equated with Wagner's aesthetic theory – ambiguity is one of the central categories.

2

The gods are in decline from the very beginning of the *Ring*. The radiance of Valhalla is a deception worked by the music, and it does not do to listen too carefully. Wagner was apparently responsible for restoring the Germanic gods to glory in the consciousness of the late nineteenth and the twentieth centuries, but in his tetralogy the myth appears in a half-light.

In the early part of the nineteenth century Germanic legend was the province of philologists; it was not part of the culture the average well-read person was expected to share with others, and it was an unusual source for opera. The *opera seria* of the seventeenth and eighteenth centuries, from Monteverdi's *Orfeo* to Mozart's *La clemenza di Tito*, plundered classical myth and Roman history for its political-cum-erotic subject matter, while by the early nineteenth century the field had expanded to admit modern history (*Les Huguenots*) and even the present day (*Fidelio*), as well as fairy-tale and exotic subjects (*Undine, Jessonda*).

People seem to have been tired of mythological operas, though agreeing that *il meraviglioso*, the unreal, 'marvellous' character of myth, was well suited to the 'unrealism' of sung drama. Singing is a natural language in *Orfeo*, but hardly in *La traviata*, which has a novelettish and, in its day, contemporary subject, though the passing of time has made it more 'operatic' than it was. Wanting something 'purely human', that is, wanting to transcend the conventions of prosaic naturalism imposed by a modern subject, Wagner was right to turn to myth for subject matter which would justify the use of a musical genre. Around 1850, to choose Germanic myth, rather than the well-worn, hackneyed myths of Greece and Rome, was a good idea on the part of an experienced librettist rather than a call to arms against the nineteenth century.

The most assiduous student of language and literature who ever wrote a libretto, Wagner completely reshaped the myth to make it his own and compliant to his operatic ends. (He accused librettists who professed to imitate him of a lack of root-and-branch thoroughness.) Yet it would be wrong to say that he 'restored' the gods of Germanic myth: he may be to blame for the dangerous political-cum-mythological nonsense that attached itself to the *Ring*, but he did not intend it. To adapt the title of Karl Reinhardt's book on Aeschylus (*Äschylos als Regisseur und Theologe*), Wagner was a theatrical producer and an *anti*-theologian. He set the divine myth to music and put it on the stage; but Ludwig Feuerbach would have entirely approved of how he portrayed it: the gods are under sentence of death, even if they do not know it. Wotan is powerless, a god whose day is done. So the myth is not so much restored by Wagner as destroyed, or, rather, it is restored in order to be destroyed. If he conjures the gods it is not to glorify them but to render them up to self-destruction, in the words of the 1848 prose sketch, 'faced with the freedom of the human consciousness'. The dead gods return in order to die again.

But even the heroic myth, contrary to Wagner's intention, occupies the same twilight area. It is hard to share Wagner's (and Nietzsche's) enthusiasm for the figure of young Siegfried. Is he the realization of the 'purely human', the forerunner of 'the human being of the future' that Wagner saw in him? Or is he not, rather, without mincing words, an insensitive, foolish bully to start with and later, in *Götterdämmerung*, a would-be deceiver who is himself deceived? The hero is not heroic, but that should not be ascribed to mischance or a weakness in the dramatic construction; it means that Wagner's conviction that the goal of history, the crowning fulfilment of human aspirations, was already comprised in our primeval origins, and that we must therefore return to myth in order to be able to form a true picture of the future, was deceptive. If Siegfried represents a Utopia, it is an unwelcome one.

3

According to the theory Wagner outlined in *Opera and Drama* (a theory that anticipated and preceded the composition of the *Ring*), the 'recurrence of melodic elements' creates the principle behind 'a unified artistic form which spreads not merely over limited areas of the drama, but over the whole drama, linking it all together'. The 'confined melody' of the traditional kind of aria was to be expanded into the 'endless melody' that embraces a whole work. The feasibility of extending a motivic association over the whole of a four-part work without monotony ensuing depends on the quantity and interest of the motives available. (Exegetes have counted and labelled more than a hundred motives in the *Ring*, not counting insignificant variants.) But Wagner never actually expressed in so many words the need for a comprehensive and varied supply of motives, obvious though it might seem, because it was countered by the desirability of limiting their number to facilitate immediate comprehension. It is a widely held and virtually ineradicable dogma that Wagner was a musical demagogue, but in fact his wish was not so much to persuade or even browbeat his listeners as to be understood; it was for that reason that he was such an indefatigable pamphleteer and speechmaker, never abandoning the hope of making himself intelligible. For him, understanding something meant recognizing the causes and motives underlying and justifying it. The central maxim of Wagner's aesthetic theory is that music, musical form, if it is to communicate something, needs a 'formal' motive: a reason for its existence. (The idea of 'absolute' music, conveying nothing beyond itself, was something he could not countenance.) The 'formal motive' of a 'melodic element' lies either in speech or in physical action or gesture: Wagner explained symphonic music, even Beethoven's, as 'idealized dance', its 'formal motive' being the movements of dancing. So two things are essential, if the use of 'melodic elements' – the leitmotive of musical drama – is to remain within the bounds of comprehension: firstly the number of motives must be small enough for the listener to keep track of them; and secondly the music must have a foundation on the stage, either in the text, in a gesture made by a character, or in an event. (When the Sword motive is first stated at the end of *Rheingold*, signalling Wotan's 'great idea' of a hero's 'freest deed', it lacks either verbal or visual motivation; Wagner thought of having Wotan pick up a sword left behind from the hoard, and, inept though the idea may have been, it illustrates his obsessional desire to have everything fully justified and explained to the point of obviousness: his musical imagination never operated in isolation from his gift for scenic visualization.)

Ready recognition and dramatic motivation are thus essential ingredients of Wagner's idea of musico-dramatic intelligibility. He wrote in *Opera and Drama:*

> These melodic elements [will] necessarily flower only at the behest of the most important dramatic motives

– Wagner always inclined towards limitation, which to him meant poetic concentration as opposed to prosaic expansion –

> and the most important of them will in turn correspond in number to those compressed, reinforced, fundamental motives

of the equally reinforced and compressed action which the poet has selected to be the pillars of his dramatic edifice; as a fundamental principle he will not employ them in bewildering multiplicity, but in the small numbers which are necessary to allow easy recognition and lend themselves to plastic formations.

In one respect the motives of the spear and the sword represent stage props and visible gestures (the Spear motive suggests someone striding forward with the point of the weapon levelled ready for use, and the Sword motive the action of drawing a sword):

In another respect they are the symbols of the 'world of contracts' and the 'realm of freedom' respectively, symbols to which the 'fundamental motives' of the drama have been 'compressed'.

Thus, while the 'melodic elements' had to be plentiful if the complex of motivic associations was to spread over the entire drama instead of just over limited parts of it, on the other hand their number had to be limited if the symphonic–dramatic form was to be immediately intelligible. The dilemma was at once aesthetic and technical and it is reasonable to suppose that it was one of the reasons why the composition of the tetralogy was delayed for so many years. Wagner felt oppressed and paralysed by the problem. Release came with the idea of developing the multitude of motives he needed from a small number of primal motives, and he recognized this as the decisive innovation introduced by leitmotivic technique. In his *Epilogic Account* of the writing of the *Ring* he wrote:

> In *Das Rheingold* I at once set out along the new path where the first thing I had to find was the plastic nature motives, which shaped themselves, as they developed in ever more individual ways, into the vehicles for the promptings of the passions motivating the much-ramified action and the characters who expressed themselves in it.

The technique of deriving motives from primal motives reconciles the conflicting requirements of limitation and abundance and this, after recognizability and dramatic motivation, is the third essential ingredient of intelligibility: a complicated motive with ramified associations remains within reach of aural comprehension, because the stages of its development out of something initially simple have been followed in the music; recognizing the origin and genealogy of a leitmotiv, the listener understands its meaning and metaphorical content.

For more than a century Wagner's 'poetic intention' and the musico-dramatic interrelationship of leitmotive have been the subject of strenuous exegetic exercises which have frequently taken off in directions suggested by fertile imaginations and tend to require rebuttal rather than further exploration. It is perhaps enough to outline some motivic associations which on the one hand are beyond the realm of speculation and on the other have some significance for the overt meaning of the work and not for the underlying meaning alone.

The Nature motive (1), a musical image of the elemental, of the primeval origins of the physical world, consists of simple sound waves derived from the broken chord of E♭ major, which go on for the 136 bars of the *Rheingold* prelude in sublime 'monotony'. Erda's motive (2), the musical emblem of the earth-mother-goddess, is simply a minor variant of the Nature motive. The rhythmic diminution of Erda's motive, the motive of Wotan's restless wandering (3), symbolizes the fear that overcomes Wotan as a result of Erda's warning of the gods' doom; the diminution, expressing haste, is a psychological element, the association with Erda is conceptual. Upward movement means evolution, downward means decline: inversion of the Nature motive produces the motive of the gods' downfall (4), whose ostensible major-mode brightness is clouded by the fact that it is often presented as the flattened (that is, darkened) supertonic in the tonal context of a minor key. The song of the Rhinemaidens (5) is derived from the Nature motive but differs from the simple broken triad in that its first note is an appoggiatura: it suggests dissonance, a characterizing divergence from the simplicity of the elemental. The Woodbird's motive (6), like the Rhinemaidens' song, the musical expression of a natural being, is a simple rhythmic variant of 5. The dissonance suggested by the first note of 5 appears, extended for emphasis, as a ninth in the first chord of the 'Rheingold!' cry (7). The Servitude motive (8a, b) is a variant of the 'Rheingold!' cry, darkened chromatically and emotively to express the Nibelungs' oppression under the ring forged from the gold.

In a letter to Brahms Wagner boasted, not without a tinge of irony, of his ability 'to construct all kinds of musical thematic material from the scenery set up in *Das Rheingold*'. Scenery? The 'plastic nature motives', out of which the musical 'vehicles for the promptings of the passions' evolve, are the images of elemental forces, of water and fire, or of landscapes, of river beds and mountain tops. But Wagner's conception of the elements and the landscapes was anthropomorphic, and it was only thus that he could represent them musically. A musical scene-painter was precisely what he was not. The images of natural phenomena – the flowing water of the *Rheingold* prelude, the tongues of flame in Loge's motive – are psychograms. And since Wagner's view of nature was anthropomorphic he could reverse the lens without any incongruity and develop motives depicting character out of nature motives.

As Nietzsche wrote:

> One can say, as a general comment on Wagner as a musician, that he has given a language to everything in nature that until now has made no attempt to speak; he does not believe that some things must inevitably be dumb. He plunges even into dawn and sunrise, into forests, fog, ravines, mountain peaks, the dead of night and moonlight, and discovers a secret longing in all of them: they want a voice.

Die Walküre

1

The action of *Die Walküre* is pieced together from the Wälsung tragedy and the Wotan myth. As a drama it is disjointed, whether considered as a work on its own or as a part of the tetralogy. The overwhelming spell it exerts over almost everybody emanates less from the whole, for it is no whole, than from individual acts, the first and the third, which are so perfectly integrated in musico-dramatic terms as to justify applying the criteria of closed dramatic form rather than those of open form. (There is no mistaking this, however classicist one's preconceptions may be.)

Dramatically, there is no real connection between the divine myth and the heroic drama, although they are linked in theory. The tragedy of the incestuous love of Siegmund and Sieglinde; the antagonism between Siegmund and Hunding, the vagrant and the settled man, each of whom is right in the opinion he holds of the other; the refusal of Siegmund, the outlaw, to share the glory of Valhalla if Sieglinde is not allowed to join him there; Siegmund's death, the necessity of which lies more in the dramatic structure, which permits no other outcome, than in the reversal of Wotan's will: very nearly every motive in the Wälsung drama is conceivable without reference to the divine myth, which does not so much provide the background and foundation of the human action as cast a penumbra round it. Siegmund's finding of the sword left for him by Wotan is as peripheral to the Wälsung drama as it is central and decisive to the future development of the dilemma in which Wotan finds himself in consequence of his 'great idea'.

It may seem, indeed, that the Wälsung tragedy provides a dramatic substance on which the myth battens; without it there would be no events to involve Wotan, Fricka and Brünnhilde. But this is deceptive: for Wotan's dialectical dilemma, the recognition that as 'lord of contracts' he on the one hand needs the hero's 'freest deed' and on the other hand is compelled to prevent it, could be demonstrated without the enactment of the Wälsung drama on the stage. The role played by the love of Siegmund and Sieglinde in the complex of motivations underlying Wotan's tragedy is illustrative, not essential.

The ideas and arguments that ought to have ensured the coherence of the heterogeneous spheres of action proved impossible to present on the stage without some structural weaknesses. *Die Walküre* is Wotan's drama — that is the only viewpoint from which the work can take on the appearance of unity — yet not a drama at all, insofar as essentially it contracts into a single moment, that at which Wotan recognizes that there is no solution to his dilemma. The Wotan action in *Die Walküre* is a monodrama or a psychodrama (which is why attention centres on the Wälsung drama in the theatre, though that is the less important so far as concepts are concerned); Brünnhilde and Fricka almost fade to allegorical figures representing the two different forces at war in Wotan. If Brünnhilde is his will — a will that turns against itself and tries to rescue Siegmund, who it knows must be sacrificed — Fricka is his conscience, forcing him to recognize the contradiction which he has tried to ignore; Wotan has to yield to Fricka because she says aloud what, without admitting it to himself, he knows in his heart of hearts to be true. Allegorizing characters in this way is more appropriate to musical drama than to spoken, where it may tend to alienate the listener; there is no difference in music between the personification of an emotion or an idea and the direct expression of it.

Brünnhilde is Wotan's will in two senses. Firstly she represents the longing to give way to an emotional urging, which Wotan has to suppress in himself.

> So tatest du,
> was so gern zu tun ich begehrt –
> doch was nicht zu tun
> die Not zwiefach mich zwang?

> '*So you did what I longed so dearly to do, but which necessity doubly compelled me not to do?*'

On the other hand Brünnhilde enables Wotan's will to extend beyond his own reach. While Wotan resigns himself to the end and directs his will to welcoming it – 'und für das Ende sorgt Alberich' – Brünnhilde lives in the expectation of a happier future (and although the gods' rule comes to an end the ring will not fall into Alberich's hands again). Though Siegmund has perished, unable, as Wotan's tool, to perform the 'freest deed', she knows his as yet unborn son Siegfried will do it. Wotan retreats into stubborn hopelessness:

> Schweig von dem Wälsungenstamm!
> Von dir geschieden
> schied ich von ihm:
> vernichten mußt' ihn der Neid.

> *'Don't name the Wälsungs to me! Turning from you I have turned from them: a malevolent fate destroyed them.'*

But Wotan's rejection of the Wälsungs, in a reversal of the dialectic that brought about Siegmund's doom, is precisely what is necessary to allow Siegfried to realize the hopes that Wotan now abandons: without Wotan's tutelage Siegfried is 'free of divine laws', whereas Siegmund, spurred on by Wotan to break those laws, fell foul of them.

2

On 3 October 1855 Wagner wrote to Liszt about *Die Walküre*:

> I am worried about the second act and the sheer dramatic weight of it: it contains two catastrophes, which are so important and so severe that they would really serve for an act each; but they are so dependent on each other, and the one draws the other after it so immediately, that it would be quite impossible to separate them.

The 'catastrophes' he was referring to, Wotan's despairing renunciation and Siegmund's death, are indeed 'dependent on each other', but conceptually and in the context of the whole tetralogy rather than dramatically and in the immediate action. Siegmund knows nothing about Wotan. The fact that it is Wotan's spear on which Siegmund's sword shatters does not affect the character of the Wälsung drama, which is complete in itself. Wotan really does no more than carry out the sentence fixed by the formal laws of tragedy.

> At times of dispassion and despondency I was frightened most of all about Wotan's long scene, in particular his revelation to Brünnhilde of the whole fateful history;

– the narrative section, beginning 'Als junger Liebe Lust mir verblich' –

> indeed, there was a moment in London when I was ready to throw the whole scene out; in order to make up my mind, I picked up the [composition] sketch once more and sang the scene through to myself with all the necessary expression; fortunately I found in doing so that my spleen was unjustified and that, on the contrary, the appropriate delivery made it riveting, even considered purely as music.

Wagner's qualms were not unreasonable; there have always been those, even among music drama's most fervent adherents, who find that the scene for Wotan and Brünnhilde in the second act hangs fire, even though it is, in Wagner's opinion, 'the most important scene for the evolution of the whole, great four-part drama'.

Ostensibly dialogue, the scene is essentially a monologue. Wotan speaks to Brünnhilde as if he was talking to himself. The weakness is rooted in the anomaly that the form is recitative, although as a monologue – according to the rules of operatic aesthetics – it has no business to be. (The theory that the distinction between recitative and aria or arioso is completely annulled in Wagner's 'endless melody' is one of those dogmas which by over-insistence turn insight into error; the difference is certainly diminished in music drama but not wiped out, and far from being a tiresome relic of traditional form, it plays a structural role.) The idea that the relationship between music and action is complementary – i.e. that the action on the stage should proceed apace during passages of recitative with its lack of melodic interest and, vice versa, that the action should be suspended during the lyric expansion of aria – is one of the maxims of traditional operatic theory which are so deeply implanted in audiences' habits of aesthetic response that they are taken for immutable laws of musical drama. (The 'action aria' was not unknown, especially in *opera buffa*, but the very fact that it was called by a special name shows it was recognized as an exception.)

Wagner's offence against the accustomed rules of operatic aesthetics – which are all the more powerful for being largely unconscious – is thus obvious: since nothing is happening on the stage during Wotan's monologue it ought to be arioso, but it is more of a recitative, breaking occasionally into arioso. But although the scene's lack of dramatic fire might seem to demonstrate the relevance of the aesthetic rules, they should be examined more closely.

Firstly, the equation of 'drama' with strenuous or decisive action –

the idea that narration and reflection are 'undramatic' – is as wrong as it is popular. The formal laws of drama – at least of the closed form in which Wagner was still working – demand that events and their motivation should be so connnected that they move towards a goal, a catastrophe or a climax. But if the audience is to grasp the connection it is necessary for the action to stand still occasionally and allow time for reflection on what has happened and consideration of what is to come. So moments of reflection are thoroughly dramatic and not epic, and that applies to musical drama quite as much as to spoken.

Secondly, in musical drama it is precisely in passages of narration and reflection that comprehension of the present time, memory of the past and presentiment of the future mingle and interpenetrate; that is, it is there that the 'associative magic' of leitmotivic technique, characterized by Wagner in *Opera and Drama* as the musical expression of memories and presentiments, has the opportunity to unfold. That is what makes every bar of Waltraute's narration in the first act of *Götterdämmerung*, which is thematically very closely linked with Wotan's monologue, 'riveting purely as music'. And that prompts the question why the construction of a dense web of motivic association, so successful in *Götterdämmerung*, fails under very similar premisses in *Die Walküre*.

It seems to be the visible – as it were, human – presence of the god which detracts from the dramatic power of the musical motivic material, the function of which is to recall the divine myth and its intervention in events *from above*. (Of course, things are different in *Das Rheingold*, the expository part of the tetralogy, insofar as the gods and the myth are presented without reference to any action involving human beings, but this is not the case in *Die Walküre*.) The motives of restlessness and discontent (the latter described by Robert Donington as 'Wotan's Will Frustrated') express Wotan's frame of mind in a situation in which the god is manifestly less than divine. So they are developed expansively and in some parts of the monologue create symphonic associations. But the motives associated with the gods and the myth that predominate elsewhere – the motives of Erda, Valhalla and the ring – appear as sporadic quotations, summoned up by specific verbal references, but without musical motivation or consequence. They are diminished because, rather than recalling the power of unseen gods, they occur in association with a visible god who is powerless to help himself. It is as though the difference between the dramatic significance of the Valhalla motive when it intervenes in the action of the first act and the pallid quotational character of the same motive in the second act struck Wagner as eroding the musical substance, and induced him not to extend the motive over any length. This causes gaps in the musical fabric, filled in by the recitative-like declamation, which creates the impression of monotony from which the scene suffers.

3

It would be mistaken to suppose that music drama shed all traces of opera, of the alternation between simple and dramatic recitative, arioso and aria. (Tradition is almost always the most powerful factor in musical reality, as in every other kind of reality.) That is not said in support of the kind of narrow-minded listeners who fail to recognize what is new in music drama and cling to the relics of what is old, so as not to come away completely empty; such listeners, unable to comprehend anything else of the 'endless melody', pick out isolated lyrical passages and commend them alone as music to enjoy, while writing off the remainder, which is the crucially important element, as a mere foil, an indistinct background. On the other hand, to ignore the presence of degrees that to some extent recall the division of a scene in opera into recitatives, ariosos and arias would merely be to exchange one kind of simplistic listening – the search for lyrical passages – for another – the immersion in an undifferentiated stream of music. Admitting the stylistic differ-entiation – which is in any case inescapable – does not do music drama an aesthetic injustice, nor is translating the innovations back into familiar, traditional terms intended to distort them or deny their validity. But the differentiation within endless melody must be recognized before the form can be understood. That endless melody is a form was something Wagner repeatedly stressed, even if he scorned to analyse his own works. Differentiation is not the brutal, pedantic division of what is essentially indivisible, but the means of distinguishing parts for the sake of the whole: articulation is what makes a form discernible.

Wagner described melody in music drama as the 'language of words-and-music' ('Wort-Ton-Sprache'). The two elements are incon-ceivable existing independently of each other: the text is meaningless without the music, and the music without the words. It is obvious enough that recitative in music drama is a structure compounded of words and music together, and not a primarily musical form; but the same must also be recognized of aria, or what takes the place of aria, in music drama. Fricka's complaint 'O, was klag' ich um Ehe und Eid', the musical culmination of her scene with Wotan at the beginning of the second act, is and is not an aria. It has the appearance of one, because it stands out from the context of their dialogue as a closed, melodic arioso complex. Its completeness is not the outcome of the grouping of conforming and contrasting melodic components according to a blueprint of musical form, however, but is essentially a matter of musical rhetoric. The complaint is made up of four sections of approximately equal length (17 + 16 + 15 + 16 bars), and its outlines are therefore immediately recognizable. (Quantity in musical syntax is synonymous with quality.) The first and second sections are analogous in the text, especially in the rhetorical attitude; the fact that the second begins with the same melodic phrase as the first underlines the verbal parallelism. The correspondence lasts for only three bars, which is too slight to justify a claim of formal repetition (A^1 A^2, as it were) on musical grounds alone, but in combination with the text and the attitude expressed it establishes a formal connection. The third section is an antithesis ('Doch jetzt'), the fourth a conclusion ('So führ' es denn aus'): the concept of the conclusion as a category of musical form was introduced by Wagner, in theory as well as practice. It would be irrelevant to describe this as, say, A^1 A^2 B C, according to the conventional terminology, because that would say nothing more than that the third and fourth sections differ from each other and from the first two sections. (The attempt to combine the 'B' and 'C' sections, so as to be able to say the passage is in Bar-form and thus musically integrated, does violence to the form.) It is only when the musical analysis adopts the categories of rhetoric, such as parallelism, antithesis and conclusion, that Fricka's complaint can be satisfyingly analysed.

In music drama recitative and aria – or their substitutes – proceed from the same principle, 'the language of words-and-music', instead of appearing in opposition to each other as distinct forms with the different functions of, respectively, action and contemplation or reflection. This fact is the foundation of the stylistic unity meant by the expression 'endless melody': that unity does not, however, exclude differentiation but rather implies it, for in a scene like that between Wotan and Fricka the contrasts between arioso and recitative passages are still marked enough to perform a structural function. The form as a whole has in turn a dramaturgical foundation: it is in the nature of the dialogue that Fricka has recourse to the histrionic attitude of rhetoric. And so Wagner neither abandoned traditional opera's principle of contrast nor adopted it in its entirety, but reconstituted it under the different premises of the 'language of words-and-music'.

Siegfried

1

Only a few days pass between the beginning of *Siegfried*, when Siegfried forges a new sword from the fragments of Nothung, and the end of *Götterdämmerung*, when Valhalla burns down: the two works come very close to fulfilling the classical postulate of unity of time. But short as the period is when measured by external time, the internal span is immeasurable. The Siegfried of *Götterdämmerung* – from the very first, not just from the moment when the magic potion alienates him from his true nature – is separated from the young dragon-killer of *Siegfried* by a gulf that could hardly be deeper: a gulf expressed musically, for instance, by the difference between Siegfried's innocent horn call and the portentous Hero theme that it becomes in *Götterdämmerung*, in which the clank of chain-mail is almost audible.

Siegfried takes place in a world that contrasts with, and complements, the tragic myth governing and weighing down upon the action of *Götterdämmerung: Siegfried* is a fairy tale. The 'shock' it gave Wagner to recognize the similarity, indeed the identity, of young Siegfried and the boy in the Grimms' fairy tale 'who leaves home to learn fear' (as he told Theodor Uhlig in May 1851) was the shock of an intuition which without warning determines the tone and character of a work once and for all.

Recognizing the fairy-tale character of *Siegfried* makes it possible to be more precise about the interval, in terms of internal time, between it and *Götterdämmerung*. Unlike sagas or legends, fairy tales take place outside historical or mythic time: never and nowhere or always and everywhere. The timelessness of fairy tale, as opposed to the temporal setting of myth, creates a separation between *Siegfried* and *Götterdämmerung* that nothing can bridge. True, the scenes in which Wotan as Wanderer discourses with Mime, Alberich and finally Siegfried serve to link the events of the fairy tale with the mythic action, and thus to bring the fairy-tale time close to that of the myth; but for one thing Siegfried, in his boyish stupidity, is shielded from the world of the mythic tragedy by the fact that he does not sense it, much less understand it, when he comes into contact with it; and for another thing Wotan, who goes about as a 'wanderer', as the ghost of himself, has withdrawn from the action by his 'negation of self' and now exists in the kind of timelessness that belongs to contemplation.

The difference from *Götterdämmerung* – as well as from *Die Walküre* – is also audible in the music, even in the particulars. Characteristic motives of *Siegfried*, the Forest Murmurs, the song of the Woodbird and Siegfried's horn call, in a sense block the musical passage of time and are at odds with the progress of cadential harmony towards a goal. They do not press forwards but persist in their own being, and thus come to express a state of nature, outside history.

Young Siegfried is a typical fairy-tale hero, without memory or inhibitions and therefore called upon to face dangers and experience marvels which he hardly recognizes as such. Conversely, the fact that the natural and the supernatural mingle without distinctions is an essential quality of fairy tale, but in order for what is marvellous to happen as if it were natural, in order for the language of birds to be as easy to understand as that of the dragon, who is really a giant, the fairy tale must have its typical hero, whose 'stupidity' gives him the entrée to this 'second' reality. (It is equally a fairy-tale trait that Siegfried does not use the treasure that comes his way: in fairy tales power and wealth are insignia, brilliant embellishments, rather than advantages for active exploitation; the important thing is obtaining them, not using them.)

Timeless though a fairy tale may be, it has its frontiers. The waking of Brünnhilde, just like that of the Sleeping Beauty, marks an ending that admits no future development because it represents perfection and fulfilment. This particular fairy tale does have a sequel, but it takes place outside the world of the fairy tale and destroys it. The fairy tale of young Siegfried is like one of the Fortunate Islands, which is swallowed up by the myth.

2

Musical forms are not merely schemata that can be represented by a sequence of letters of the alphabet but possess their individual characters, stamped by the kinds of melodic and thematic material that are appropriate and historically possible at the time of composition. The basic patterns of song and rondo form, A B A and A B A C A, depend on contrast (AB and AC) and repetition (of A after B or C); the parts must be relatively complete in themselves as well as easily distinguishable from each other, if the constituency of any one part is not to conflict with the nature of the whole, which relies on grouping, not development. Song and rondo form are, metaphorically speaking, 'architectonic' not 'logical'. A rondo ritornello that evinced differentiation and contrast within itself would defeat its own function, because that kind of thematic material demands development and elaboration; the marked caesura between the ritornello and the succeeding episode would seem to break off a musical argument rather than to perform its normal articulatory function, and when the ritornello was repeated unchanged it would disappoint by appearing to have missed the opportunity for development, instead of being recognized as obeying the principle of architectonic symmetry. (The strengths of logical form are the weaknesses of architectonic form, and vice versa.) But the effect the form thus has on the nature of the melodic and thematic material has consequences for the musical content. Not every form is appropriate to every kind of content; it would be foolish to attempt to express something complicated or abstruse in song or rondo form. The inescapable, fundamental characteristic of repetitive forms is simplicity. And so it is not a fluke, but a testimony to Wagner's sense of form, that in *Siegfried*, which is a fairy-tale opera rather than a heroic myth, the dialogue continually shapes itself into song and rondo forms, without such forms having been prefigured in the text: the musical forms have something to say in their own characters, regardless of the content of the words they set.

In the expository first scene between Mime and Siegfried, where the fairy-tale atmosphere is almost completely unalloyed, a number of songs can be isolated without doing violence to the structure. Their simplicity of form makes them stand out in the dramatic–symphonic context, and

Wagner clearly took pains to strike in them the authentic note, whether the song is parody, like Mime's 'starling's song', 'Als zullendes Kind zog ich dich auf', or artless and straightforward, like Siegfried's 'Es sangen die Vöglein so selig im Lenz'. (The naivety is of course artificial, but that does not detract from it in the least; it is tempting, on the contrary, to describe this 'second' immediacy as more 'authentic' than if it were an immediacy encountered in its 'first' stage.)

Some of the scene's song-structures are modified by a tendency towards developmental form, i.e. towards a 'logical' formal principle; this blending of the apparently incompatible is not a fault but makes a musico–dramatic point. Mime's song 'Jammernd verlangen Junge', which has four sections in an $A^1 A^2 B A^3$ pattern, and Siegfried's 'Es sangen die Vöglein', which consists of two strophic stanzas, are not simply juxtaposed without any connection between them, but share a ritornello, which the exegetes have defined as the motive expressing Siegfried's longing for love.

In Mime's song the ritornello comes as an interpolation, as if Mime is seeking to hold at bay a thought that is urging itself on him. It is only in Siegfried's strophic song that it unfolds, expansive and emphatic, in the orchestral accompaniment. The way the motive is worked, by means of the traditional development techniques of sequence and separation of the motive's parts, is undeniably inconsistent with simple strophic form, but far from being a dead, negative contradiction it is motivated and eloquent. In the event the song benefits, both musically and dramatically, from allowing developmental techniques to encroach on its formal structure: it is enhanced musically by the differentiated chromatic treatment of the motive, which demands or at least suggests musical development; and its dramatic role is heightened by the separation of the conscious and the unconscious, reflected by the stylistic contrast between the vocal and the instrumental melodies. The chromaticism, as the musical symbol of unconscious impulses, counters the naivety implicit in the song form. The difference in character between the vocal and instrumental melodies gives the form a dual, even ambiguous, aspect, inasmuch as it is song form in the vocal part and development form in the orchestra.

3

In a mood of resignation and some disillusion, Wagner wrote to Liszt on 28 June 1857 that he had broken off the composition of *Siegfried* in the middle of the second act.

> I have guided my young Siegfried as far as the beautiful solitude of the forest; there I have left him under the linden tree and have bidden him farewell with heartfelt tears: he is better off there than anywhere else.

(He meant that he had abandoned the composition sketch eight bars into the Forest Murmurs, before Siegfried's 'Daß der mein Vater nicht ist, wie fühl' ich mich drob so froh'.)

Wagner was by temperament a man to persist doggedly to the end in anything he had once undertaken. It is all the more amazing that he decided to abandon *Siegfried* when external pressures on him, intolerable as they were, were no worse than they had been for several years. In fact, he changed his mind to the extent of finishing the sketch of the second act within the next few weeks. He wrote to Princess Marie Wittgenstein in August 1857:

> After a break, I had paper in front of me one morning, all ready to draft the text of *Tristan*, when I was suddenly overpowered by such a yearning anxiety about Siegfried that I got him out again and decided to finish his second act at least. That has now been done: Fafner is dead, Mime is dead and Siegfried has run off after the Woodbird as it flutters away.

The work lay unfinished for twelve years, until 1869. Only once in all that time, in July 1859, is there any allusion to a musical idea for *Siegfried*. He was working on the third act of *Tristan* when it occurred to him that a melodic phrase he had thought of 'did not belong to Tristan's Shepherd but Siegfried himself', and so what might have been the Shepherd's 'merry tune' was given to the words in the final duet in the third act of *Siegfried*, 'Sie ist mir ewig, ist mir immer Erb und Eigen, Ein und All'' (see below).

It is not clear why Wagner broke off the composition of *Siegfried*, without being certain whether he would ever complete it, or be able to perform *Das Rheingold* and *Die Walküre* as fragments of the tetralogy. He seems to have been obsessed in 1857 with the idea of a popular work which would break down his ever more oppressive sense of being isolated from the rest of the world. (In 1857 he had the bizarre and self-deluding idea of writing *Tristan* to an Italian libretto and making a simple opera of it.) After the first act of *Siegfried* was finished, he wrote to Julie Ritter in May 1857 that he was convinced that it had the greatest popular appeal of all his works and would very quickly be established in the repertory, with the result that it would draw the other parts of the tetralogy in its wake, one by one, He was wrong: *Siegfried* has never become as popular as *Die Walküre*. More significant than that, however, is that he considered launching *Siegfried* on its own, because of what he believed to be its potential popularity, and appears to have been ready to abandon the idea of performing the tetralogy only, or primarily, as a complete cycle. It cannot have been long before he realized that the hopes he entertained of *Siegfried* were illusory, and perhaps the resignation that overpowered him in June 1857 was connected with a recognition that the third act, where the action leaves the fairy tale and enters the myth, was irreconcilable with the idea of the work as popular and self-sufficient.

The difference between the fairy tale and the myth, between the Woodbird's scene in the second act and Wotan's conjuration of Erda at the beginning of the third, is abrupt and extreme, though Wagner made an obvious effort to mediate between the two separate worlds, through the insertion of Wotan's scenes with Mime in the first act and with Alberich in the second, which are otherwise only weakly motivated in terms of the dramatic structure. The work's unity was already endangered; interruption of the composition by an interval in which *Tristan* and *Meistersinger* were written could have been expected to lead inevitably to its complete collapse. The amazing thing is that Wagner managed to preserve the score from any such collapse; the use of leitmotive from a common store in the different parts of the work was sufficient to prevent a sense of discontinuity being created by the stylistic divergence. *Tristan* and *Meistersinger* have left clear stylistic marks on the third act of *Siegfried*, but there can be no question of a breach in the unity of the work, even if that unity is an artificial construct.

The style of *Tristan* – the peripeteia, if not quite the catastrophe, of the history of music in the nineteenth century – is recalled in the third act of *Siegfried* by, for instance, the motive at Siegfried's words 'Noch bist du mir die träumende Maid'.

Listened to more exactly, more analytically, the motive can be deciphered as a chromatic variant of the theme that expresses the love of Siegfried and Brünnhilde.

The chromaticization transforms the extrovert character of the theme into its opposite; as in the second act of *Tristan*, the music seems to retreat from the world, to withdraw from the appearance into the essence, of which music is the image in sound, according to Schopenhauer.

To give an example of a technical particular that has a profound aesthetic significance, the treatment of the dissonance in this quotation from *Siegfried* is characteristic of the style of *Tristan*. The extended dissonance on A♮ ('mir') is resolved, not on to a consonance, but on to yet another dissonance, the passing-note B♭, and the supporting seventh chord moves on to another seventh chord instead of to a triad. So the accent is on dissonances, on non-resolution. Consonance is present only as the unspoken thought in the background: the identity and allegorical or expressive significance of dissonance are due to the fact of its being 'determined negation' of, and divergence from, consonance, but the consonance itself does not need to be heard.

If, therefore, it is their unspoken but ever conscious relationship, as premiss or implication, to simple diatonicism and consonance that gives the chromaticism and unresolved dissonance of the style of *Tristan* their expressive character and compelling emotional effectiveness, the reverse is also the case – and this is characteristic of the style of *Meistersinger*: chromaticism and dissonance can be sensed as the unheard background to diatonicism and consonance. If, generally speaking, simplicity is the foil to complexity, in Wagner it sometimes seems that complexity provides the background to simplicity. The triumphant diatonicism of

Meistersinger, which recurs in *Siegfried* in the final duet, is a 'second' diatonicism in the same sense that Hegel spoke of 'second' nature: a diatonicism that has expanded to include chromaticism. The melody of Siegfried's words, 'Sie ist mir ewig, ist mir immer Erb und Eigen, Ein und All'', a paradigm of robust diatonicism, occurred to Wagner, as has been said, when he was composing the third act of *Tristan*, the ultimate in chromaticism.

The melody's naivety is artificial and therefore immune to the temptation to associate it with folk music.

Another feature of the style of *Meistersinger* in the last act of *Siegfried*, besides the 'second' diatonicism (with which it is closely associated), is the contrapuntalism of the finale, superimposing themes that originated independently – the motives of jubilation, love and Siegfried himself – in the upper, middle and lower parts.

There is undoubtedly a trace of violence, of forcing heterogeneous elements together, clinging to this counterpoint, and it is no accident that it was praised by Richard Strauss and criticized by that obstinately conservative theorist Heinrich Schenker. It is a musico–poetic procedure rather than a purely musical one; the decisive factor is not how the separate parts interlock (their musical interrelationship results almost entirely from the fact that they all employ pitches of the same chord) but what their combination expresses.

Götterdämmerung

1

In the tragedy that originally bore his name Siegfried is no more than a tool in Hagen's plot, playing hardly more independent a role than Gutrune and Gunther, who are saved from being boring only by their ambivalence. The leitmotive in *Götterdämmerung* that are most apt for Siegfried are the motives of the Tarnhelm and the potion of oblivion, musical enigmas composed of pallid, deceptive harmonies. Yet even the protagonist and antagonist between whom the action is really waged, Hagen and Brünnhilde, are somehow stilted and incomplete as characters: they are not much more than the vessels for certain unmitigated passions. Hagen is all ambition for the ring and the power it represents: all 'envy' as Wagner himself put it. In Brünnhilde, emphatic, unreserved love, which blots out every other consideration, switches abruptly to insensate hatred when Siegfried betrays her, only to be transformed back just as immediately into love when she sees through the treachery to which Siegfried has fallen victim. Instead of characters in any true sense of the word, these 'personages' are like arenas for the uncontrolled display of emotions that burst in upon their souls from outside, unalleviated by human characteristics.

As a consequence there is no room in the relationship between the protagonist and the antagonist for any kind of dramatic dialectical argument. Either Hagen and Brünnhilde are contrasted in every way without the least mediating factor, or else – in the conspiracy scene in the second act – they conjoin in unholy alliance. The fact that Wagner chose to cast their plotting in one of the forms he had explicitly rejected for music drama, in a duet – or trio, since Gunther is included in the conspiracy – is by no means fortuitous. A musical drama in which the characters are mere vessels for passions and the dialogue takes the form of tableaux, in which concurring or contrasting emotions are decked out with the appropriate musical colouring, is nothing other than an opera.

Yet at the same time – ambiguity being the quality that stamps the musico-dramatic character of the work – *Götterdämmerung* is a dramatic symphony: 'dramatic' not only in the superficial sense that the symphony, the 'orchestral melody', is the accompaniment to a drama, but also insofar as the symphonic function and weight are founded in the special conceptual and dramatic construction of the work: the relationship between the divine myth and the heroic drama. The scenes in which the divine myth dominates the action, the Norns' scene in the prologue, Waltraute's narration, and Hagen's dream exchange with Alberich, do not so much directly influence the course of the action as imbue the events taking place in a temporal setting with a mythic significance – providing them, as it were, with a reverberation spreading far beyond their immediate sphere – and at the same time they serve to set *Götterdämmerung*, the drama of Siegfried's death, in its proper place in the total context of the tetralogy. An analogous function falls, however, to the music as well, the symphonic 'orchestral melody', which weaves the immense background to the events from reminiscences and fleeting allusions, and whose store of mythic motives – those of the ring, Valhalla, Erda, the gods' downfall, contracts and the curse – connects the events now taking place to their primeval premises and origins. Thus, though the scenes in which the divine myth is directly referred to may seem peripheral to the dramatic structure if considered solely in respect of their contribution to the stage action, musically they are central: they create the framework for the complex of motivic associations that spreads over the whole drama. If there is any danger of the divine myth fading in significance beside the heroic drama, because it does not take physical shape on the stage, the music restores it – and the overall context of the cycle – to its rightful dramatic place.

The musico-dramatic structure of *Götterdämmerung* – the dramatic structure depending as much on the musical as the musical structure on the dramatic – is thus determined by the pivotal relationship between the divine myth and the heroic drama, between its place in the cycle and its identity as a separate work, between its musical symbolism and its stage action, between the drama as symphony and the drama as opera. The complexity is increased by the consequences of the length of time that passed between the conception of the text and the composition of the music.

2

The music of *Götterdämmerung* stretches between the two extremes of the symphonic weave of motives and the closed forms of opera: but there is mediation between those extremes, they do not simply exist alongside and unconnected. The more densely the motives seem to be woven together – and the motives of the entire tetralogy are assembled in *Götterdämmerung* – the more overpowering, on the one hand, is the listener's inclination to abandon critical awareness and attention to musical forms, and surrender to the 'associative magic', and the more essential it is therefore, on the other hand, to be conscious of the syntactic framework that stands behind the succession and concatenation of the motives and gives them form: the articulation of the 'endless melody' in rhetorical periods adapted to musical uses.

Waltraute's narration in the first act of *Götterdämmerung* ('Höre mit Sinn, was ich dir sage') is a passage in which musical motives from the divine myth crowd thickly together. It consists of seven periods short enough to be discerned as such (17 + 18 + 17 + 24 + 16 + 33 + 31 bars). This quantitative element is relevant: if confusion is to be avoided, listeners must be able to assume that constructions which they are supposed to comprehend as musical periods will remain within certain limits.

The verbal syntax and the music work together to make the periodic division of Waltraute's narration perfectly clear. Each period is dominated musically by one principal motive, which both ensures the coherence of the period as such and distinguishes it clearly from the neighbouring periods. The principal motive in the first period is that of Wotan's discontent or frustration; in the second ('Jüngst kehrte er heim') it is the Valhalla motive, chromatically distorted. Subsidiary motives – the rhythmic Valkyrie figure in the first period, the motives of the spear and the World Ash in the second – are summoned by allusions in the text and therefore have the character of quotations; they are often no more than interpolations so far as the musical form goes: they make their entrances, as Shaw complained about leitmotive in general, on cue.

The differentiation of the principal and subsidiary motives, fundamental to the understanding of the musical form, is a functional, not an essential, distinction: the principal motive of one period can turn up as a subsidiary in another. This alternation of function is even one of the means both of associating two periods – through the recurrence – and of differentiating them – through the change in status. Another means to the same dual end is the process of introducing variations on a motive that transform it into something different, in a way that leaves the relationship apparent; alternatively the process of variation can bring closer together two motives that originated independently of each other, so that one seems to have been derived from the other. The principal motive of the fifth period of Waltraute's narration ('Seine Raben beide') is the 'Rheingold' cry, both in its original form and darkened and distorted chromatically: the two forms – the second has been accorded the status of a motive in its own right and labelled 'Servitude' – are sharply contrasted and yet are felt to constitute a single principal motive in this period. In the sixth period ('Seine Knie umwindend') the 'Rheingold' cry is demoted to a subsidiary motive, an orchestral quotation, yet it is linked to the new principal motive, that of Wotan's discontent, by a common feature, the accented and prolonged downward semitone step, although the motives were not originally derived from each other. The association is secondary.

The symphonic quality of *Götterdämmerung*, the differentiation of the motivic technique, is balanced against the return, as in the third act of *Siegfried*, to traditional operatic forms: the duet at the end of *Siegfried*, the trio that closes the second act of *Götterdämmerung*. The explanation lies in the history of the work's genesis – *Siegfried* and *Götterdämmerung* were conceived first, and composed last. The use of voices of distinctly different character to form duets or trios in two- or three-part harmony was something Wagner avoided in *Rheingold* and *Walküre*, because to have characters speaking at once contradicts the dialogue principle of spoken drama, which he wanted to apply in music drama. (The Rhinemaidens or the Valkyries are hardly individualized, so if they combine in musical ensembles, in passages of text of a type which might well be sung even in a spoken play, it is compatible with the dialogue principle.) But from the third act of *Siegfried* onwards Wagner overruled his own anti-operatic aesthetic theory. His disregard for the dogmas of music drama can be at least partly explained by the fact that the texts of *Siegfried* and *Götterdämmerung* were written earlier than those of *Rheingold* and *Walküre*, at a time when the principles of music drama were not so firmly laid down as later. At all events, the traditional forms are too clearly prefigured in the texts of the Siegfried–Brünnhilde duet and the Hagen–Brünnhilde–Gunther trio, in the syntactical and semantic parallelisms which demand to be sung simultaneously, for it to have been feasible to set them as dialogue. Moreover Wagner had shown himself ready to revert from dialogue to duet in *Tristan* whenever the drama permitted it, when discourse turned into the expression of complete agreement. Similarly the duet in *Siegfried* and the trio in *Götterdämmerung* can be interpreted as expressions of agreement – whether in love or in hatred; the dramatic dialectic has been suspended. The significance of this is that the distance travelled away from the dialogue principle of music drama and towards operatic convention was essentially small, for the highest musico-dramatic capability of an operatic ensemble is the power to express contrasting views simultaneously (which would be an absurd, incomprehensible hubbub in spoken drama, yet is perfectly feasible and expressive in opera, because the music differentiates and at the same time combines the voices) but that capability is precisely what Wagner did not restore in these ensembles.

3

Wagner changed the end of *Götterdämmerung* time and again, as though there were no limit to the drastically different political and/or philosophical convictions one drama could be expected to express. This is a source of great embarrassment to exegetes who would prefer to grasp an author by his 'last words'. Wagner himself was by no means certain what his own work meant, and it is safer for us to place our trust in Wagner the dramatist than in the philosopher, who propounded the ideology of himself.

The gold has been returned to the Rhinemaidens, and the curse annulled thereby, so Utopia seems to be in the air. But the Rhinemaidens are only elemental beings: pre-human rather than human. The world of the gods, represented by Valhalla, has fallen, according to the will of Wotan, who made his own the doom that he could not escape. But nothing is known about the humans except that they have survived the catastrophe: 'From the ruins of the hall the men and women look up with rapt attention, watching the fire as it grows to fill the sky.' Does rapt attention at the sight of an old world in flames mean simultaneous awareness of the dawn of the new one?

In the 1852 version of the text there were some lines in Brünnhilde's final oration that Wagner later rejected.

Nicht Gut, nicht Gold,
noch göttliche Pracht;

nicht Haus, nicht Hof,
noch herrischer Prunk;
nicht trüber Verträge
trügender Bund,
nicht heuchelnder Sitte
hartes Gesetz:
selig in Lust und Leid
läßt – die Liebe nur sein.

'*Not goods, not gold, nor godly splendour; not house, not land, nor lordly pomp; not the cheating covenant of cheerless contracts, not the harsh laws of lying custom: rapture in pleasure and pain comes – from love alone.*'

In 1856 Wagner replaced the proclamation of a 'realm of freedom' that would arise from the ruins of the world of 'cheerless contracts' with lines in the spirit of Schopenhauer.

Aus Wunschheim zieh ich fort,
Wahnheim flieh' ich auf immer;
des ew'gen Werdens
offne Tore
schließ ich hinter mir zu:
nach dem wunsch- und wahnlos
heiligsten Wahlland,
der Weltwanderung Ziel,
von Wiedergeburt erlöst,
zieht nun die Wissende hin.
Alles Ew'gen
sel'ges Ende,
wißt ihr, wie ich's gewann?
Trauernder Liebe
tiefstes Leiden
schloß die Augen mir auf:
enden sah ich die Welt.

'*I depart from Wish-home, I flee Delusion-home for ever; I close behind me the open doors of eternal becoming: where there is no wishing or delusion, to the holiest chosen land, the goal of world-wandering, released from [the cycle of] rebirth, made wise I now go. Know you how I accomplished the blessed end of all eternal*

> things? Sorrowing love's deepest suffering opened my eyes: I saw
> the world end.'

Once again Brünnhilde is the paradigm of a future human race. But the
Utopia to which she looks forward is a negative one: reconciliation is
to be achieved only through renunciation, not through love. A world that
is nothing but predestined fate and inescapable entanglements is to end
in universal resignation and denial of the self.

In the end Wagner set neither of these alternative endings, the utopian
or the resigned. (The fact that he set the 1852 ending privately for King
Ludwig is beside the point.) He believed that the paraphrase of
Schopenhauer expressed the ending more suitably, but that the 'poetic
intention' had no need of this formulation in words, since it was
'realized' in the drama.

> Finally it could not escape the composer that, since the meaning
> of these lines was already expressed with the greatest definition
> in the tenor of the musical drama, their actual delivery had to
> be eliminated from the performance.

But he seems to have been deceived as to the meaning of his own work.
The really authentic ending is obviously the version of 1852, which was
already prefigured in the first conception, the prose sketch of 1848.

Firstly, Wagner changed his mind about the 1852 ending, though
unobtrusively. In a letter to Röckel of 23 August 1856 he described it
as 'tendentious': as distorting the drama by imposing on it a political
and philosophical view from outside, as it were, when the drama of itself
aimed in another direction. Then, when the text was published in a
volume of the *Collected Writings* in 1873, the lines were referred to only
as 'sententious': attempting, that is, to put into words what did not need
to be said, since it emerged from the action. But 'sententious' is a word
that appies equally well to the Schopenhauer paraphrase.

Secondly, the theme in the orchestra with which *Götterdämmerung*
ends is not a musical metaphor of renunciation and 'negation of the
will', but an expression of the 'rapturous love' celebrated in the 1852
ending.

The theme was first heard in *Die Walküre*, at Sieglinde's words 'O hehrstes Wunder', after Brünnhilde has foretold the birth of Siegfried.

Thirdly, the Schopenhauer paraphrase of 1856, in which Brünnhilde's renunciation – in the form of recognition of the futility of the world's course – is said to spring from 'sorrowing love's deepest suffering', is dramaturgically inadequate: it perhaps makes an ending to *Götterdämmerung* in isolation, but it will not do for the whole tetralogy. In *Götterdämmerung*, with the exception of the scene in the prologue where Siegfried and Brünnhilde bid each other farewell, love is shown, as Wagner put it in the same letter to Röckel, 'creating some pretty thorough havoc'. But in the overall context embracing the last act of *Die Walküre*, the last act of *Siegfried*, as well as the prologue and the ending of *Götterdämmerung*, Brünnhilde's love for Siegfried features as the alternative to Wotan's resignation and renunciation of the world and looks forward in hope to reconciliation in the future. In the prose sketch of 1848 Wagner had written that the gods' purpose

> will have been achieved when they have destroyed themselves in this human creation, namely when they have had to surrender their direct influence, faced with the freedom of the human consciousness.

The music Wagner wrote in 1874 to bring *Götterdämmerung* to its conclusion expresses just that. His first conception was also his last.

Parsifal

1

On 28 September 1880, still a year and a half before he finished the score of *Parsifal*, Wagner wrote to King Ludwig:

> I have now had to yield up all my works, conceived with such high ideals, to what I consider the profoundly immoral practices of our theatres and their audiences

– he meant the juxtaposition in the normal repertory of works which of their nature questioned each other's existence –

> so that I have had to ask myself seriously whether it is not my duty to preserve this last and most sacred of my works from the same fate, namely a commonplace operatic career.

Played in a normal opera season, even the 'festival drama of dedication' itself would become just another opera.

> A decisive factor I can no longer ignore, which compels me to take this view, is the purity of the subject of my *Parsifal*.

It seems from this that Wagner made a distinction of degree but not of principle between the 'most sacred' of his works and its precursors, as if *Tannhäuser*, in some respects a prototype of *Parsifal*, was also 'sacred' though to a less pronounced degree. Or is *Parsifal*, the 'festival drama of dedication' which Wagner wanted to reserve for Bayreuth (not in order to save his festival, but to protect the work), religious theatre in a sense that *Tristan* – in which the word 'God' does not once appear – is not?

Nietzsche accused Wagner, the author of the *Ring*, the anti-theological

myth of the downfall of the gods, of 'breaking down before the Cross'
in *Parsifal*. That was as perverse, and revealed as great a deficiency in
artistic understanding, as the contrary accusation that Wagner was an
unscrupulous theatromane who dissipated Christian myths and symbols
in order to make theatrical effects. The latter charge springs from a
fundamentalist acceptance of Christian dogma and contempt for the
theatre, whereas Wagner took a philosopher's view of Christianity and
regarded the theatre in the spirit of ancient Greece. The relationship of
'artistic purity' and 'engagement' is far too complicated to be resolved
in simple formulas: the idea that the intention behind a work should be
completely taken up and absorbed into the finished artistic creation so
as to leave no trace of itself is as dogmatic as the diametrically opposite
belief that the 'art' in a work serves, and should serve, only as a vehicle
for putting across a message. The premises and implications of the
argument change from one era to the next. (To take an example at the
furthest extreme from Wagner: is Brecht's Marxism a means to the end
of writing plays, as Max Frisch suspected, and a perfectly expedient
means at that, or, vice versa, is his play-writing a vehicle – practical or
otherwise – for changing things according to Marxist ideology? The
alternative, as posed, is forced: it separates things that cannot be parted.)

Wagner's faith was philosophical, not religious, a metaphysic of
compassion and renunciation, deriving its essential elements from
Schopenhauer's *World as Will and Idea* and – via Schopenhauer – from
Buddhism. Wagner found these elements also present in Christianity,
and to that extent he was a Christian. But the predominant spirit of the
nineteenth century had become alien to fundamentalist faith, and he too
took a historico-philosophical view of the traditions of the religion as
an evolving truth, changing its outer shape throughout history. The myth
that was once believed as literal truth had become a metaphor for a
metaphysical insight; and the rituals of an earlier age, grown hollow and
insubstantial as such, passed over into art, so as to preserve or recover
in a symbolic role the meaning and cogency that they had lost in their
hieratic function. In 1880 Wagner wrote in *Religion and Art*, the
philosophical complement to *Parsifal*:

> One could say that where religion is becoming artificial

– in Hegelian terms, where it ceases to be substantive –

> it is for art to salvage the nucleus of religion by appropriating
> the mythic symbols, which the former

– religion in its mythic phase –

> wished to propagate as true, for their symbolic worth, so as to reveal the truth buried deep within them by means of ideal presentation of the same.

Parsifal is therefore undeniably a document of the nineteenth-century 'religion of art'. This does not mean that art should be venerated as religion – or as pseudo-religion, for the holder of fundamentalist Christian views – and works of art worshipped as religious icons, but that religion – or its truth – has passed from the form of myth into the forms of art. The historico-philosophical hour had come for the art that, in Wagner's view, was the quintessence of all the arts: drama.

2

Parsifal is a work of summation, in which the composer gathered and joined together the threads of his past. The subject had been in his mind since the mid-1840s, since the completion of *Tannhäuser* and the conception of *Lohengrin*, and an inner connection with both those works is apparent. (There is a tendency in Wagner's oeuvre as a whole, as he himself understood it, to a mythological systematization, a poetic technique of leitmotiv that extends beyond any one individual drama.) Kundry, the 'rose of hell', is a second Venus; Klingsor's magic garden recalls the Venusberg; and the realm of the Grail fortress Monsalvat has already been prefigured, even musically, in *Lohengrin*.

On the other hand Parsifal, the 'pure fool' who has grown up in the wilderness and is called to be the saviour of a world he knows nothing about, is another Siegfried. Kundry says of him:

> Schächer und Riesen traf seine Kraft:
> den freislichen Knaben fürchten sie alle.

> '*Rogues and giants fell to his strength: they all fear the mettlesome boy.*'

But the 'will' that spurs Parsifal on to deeds of valour is broken by the coming of compassion; his goal is not the 'freest deed' but renunciation. Siegfried forges a sword so as to kill a dragon, but Parsifal breaks his bow when he realizes the sin he committed in killing the swan. Siegfried's kiss awakens Brünnhilde to 'radiant day'; Kundry's kiss makes Parsifal 'cosmically clear-sighted' ('welthellsichtig') to the things of darkness and night, to the 'delusion' that overtakes all but those who renounce the 'will' and cast off the yoke of blind urging and compulsion.

But the work with which *Parsifal* is most closely connected is undoubtedly *Tristan*. In 1854 Wagner sketched a scene in which Parsifal, as a knight errant seeking the Grail, comes to Kareol where Tristan lies mortally wounded. On 30 May 1859 Wagner wrote to Mathilde Wesendonk:

> It dawned on me recently yet again that this [*Parsifal*] is bound to be another cruel task. Strictly speaking, Amfortas is the centre and the principal subject of the work. And, you know, that's quite a story. Just think, for heaven's sake, what's involved! It has suddenly become terribly clear to me: he's my Tristan in the third act, but inconceivably intensified. Wounded by the spear and probably with another wound besides – in his heart, in his fearful agony the poor man longs for nothing but death; to obtain this ultimate relief he is constantly driven to look on the Grail again, in case it will at least close his wound, for nothing else is able to do it, nothing – nothing can help him: but time and again the Grail only gives him this same thing, the inability to die.

It was this tragic paradox, that the path undertaken on the search for salvation leads to destruction, so similar to his conception of the *Ring*, that kindled Wagner's enthusiasm for the subject. Kundry, too, is caught in an analogous trap: in her search for absolution, she yearns for Parsifal's embrace, but if Parsifal succumbs to her as Amfortas did she will only plunge even deeper into the damnation from which she is trying to escape.

> O, Elend! Aller Rettung Flucht!
> O, Weltenwahns Umnachten:
> in höchsten Heiles heißer Sucht
> nach der Verdammnis Quell zu schmachten!

> '*O misery! Flight of all deliverance! Enveloping night of world's delusion! In the heated search for the highest salvation, to thirst for the source of damnation!*'

There is also an obvious parallel between *Parsifal* and Wagner's project for a play on the life of Christ, *Jesus von Nazareth*, conceived in his Dresden years, in the scene in the third act where Kundry appears as a penitent Magdalene, Parsifal as Christ and Gurnemanz as John the Baptist. And there is also the 1856 sketch for the Buddhist drama *Die Sieger*, which prefigures the motive of Kundry's rebirth and eventual absolution.

For all the complexity of *Parsifal*'s links with earlier works and unrealized projects, the work itself, its text written in 1877 and its music completed in 1882, is simple in outline. The strict symmetry of the external form of the piece – the third act repeats the scheme of the first, while the second forms a contrast – is architectural, but it encloses an inner action that is linear, following step by step a progress described in words that act half as a motto, half as an oracular riddle: 'Durch Mitleid wissend, der reine Tor' ('The pure fool, made wise by compassion').

In the first act, in the 'holy ground' outside the Grail castle, Parsifal feels a first intimation of pity after killing the swan. (The scene with the swan is peripheral to the outer action but crucial to the inner.) On witnessing Amfortas's agony during the Grail ceremony in the castle, he feels a compulsive pain in his own heart, but he does not yet dare to put the 'redeeming question': his compassion is still dull and inarticulate. (The motivation seems to have become confused: would Amfortas be relieved of his agony if Parsifal asked the cause of it at this point? Or must he wait for the return of the spear which he lost to Klingsor when he succumbed to Kundry? 'Die Wunde schließt der Speer nur, der sie schlug.' ('Only the spear that struck it heals the wound.') The answer lies in the interrelationship of pragmatic and symbolic elements, which is the principle underlying the dramatic structure of *Parsifal*: the spear that heals the wound is to be interpreted as a symbol of compassion, 'the reversal of the will' as Schopenhauer understood it. This compassion is not a negative emotion but insight into the suffering of the world, and the only consolation for it is recognition of the lack of any consolation, in other words, resignation.) In the second act Parsifal, the 'pure fool', is made 'cosmically clear-sighted' by Kundry's kiss. He feels in himself the temptation, the longing and the suffering of Amfortas, and perceives the world as the aggregation of common guilt and an unending circle of misery, which can be broken only by compassion and renunciation, by rejection of the will and its blind urging and compulsion. The events of the third act, Kundry's baptism, Amfortas's healing and the redemption of the Grail 'from guilt-stained hands' – the hands of Amfortas as the representative of a world of entanglement and compromises – are nothing more than the fulfilment of what is already foreseeable at the end of the second, once Parsifal has regained the spear. (Parsifal's wanderings in search of the Grail, which are portrayed in the prelude to the third act, are a check on the progress of the action but do not affect the outcome.) But although this last act is 'uneventful' by the normal dramatic criteria it is not just a ritual, the mere enactment and symbolic representation of a long foregone conclusion. It presents a third stage in the inner action: the compassion that is a dull sensation in the first act, and widens into recognition, 'cosmic perception', in the second, is at last directed outwards in the third as the 'deed of redemption'. Parsifal becomes the Grail King, not an anchorite, and does not turn his back on the world. (Whether Wagner's 'theory of regeneration', supplementing and in part rebutting Schopenhauer's metaphysics of the will and renunciation, is the foundation of the dramatic construction of *Parsifal* or vice versa – that is, whether the philosophy grew out of the dramaturgy or the dramaturgy out of the philosophy – is uncertain.)

3

Parsifal, a figure from legend rather than the sagas, is a passive hero: the decisive deed that marks the drama's turning point is a refusal. The action, into the centre of which he unwittingly stumbles, is nothing but the starting point and the external aspect of his progress towards knowledge. *Parsifal* is close to being an example of that paradoxical genre, the hagiographic drama.

The dramaturgical consequences of the hero's passivity serve to distinguish the 'festival drama of dedication' from a drama. Since Parsifal does not act, nor direct himself towards a goal (except in his search for the Grail, which he finds through grace not effort), and since he comes to himself through reaction, not resolution, the prehistory of the drama has to be expounded in epic narrations, instead of being integrated in a sequence of interconnecting plots to provide early motivation for later events. As a result the narrator, Gurnemanz, a lay figure dramaturgically, has the biggest part in the work. One exception proving this rule is Kundry's telling of the tale of Herzeleide, Parsifal's mother, in the second act: ostensibly a narration of something in the past, it in fact has an important part to play in the seduction scene, which it requires the insights of psychoanalysis to interpret. (It is not inconceivable, however, that the second act of *Parsifal* and the third act of *Siegfried* exercised an unacknowledged influence on the development of psychoanalytical theory.)

The exposition scene comprising Gurnemanz's narration, and occupying the major part of the first act, is simultaneously a series of tableaux. In it the epic element is combined with visual components, whose contribution to the dramatic form is illustrative rather than structural. The reason for this additional visual material is at least partly musical, since it facilitates the comprehensible and memorable exposition of leitmotive. In his passion for clarity and absolute intelligibility, Wagner was in general unsatisfied if the meaning of a new leitmotiv was represented only in the text; if it was at all possible he accompanied it with something visible on the stage. This visual factor did not have to be an advance in the action; it could just as well be a tableau.

The first statements of the Grail and Faith motives are not made in response to a verbal cue: they are heard as offstage music, a reveille, in a scene of prayer which illustrates the nature of the Grail kingdom with hardly a word spoken.

Kundry's motives, the galloping figure and the violent descending figure suggestive of collapse, are musical illustrations of her mode of entry.

Instead of merely hearing about Amfortas from Gurnemanz, we see him carried across the stage on his litter. The only thing that happens in the short scene is that he receives from Kundry a herb which will not heal him, but it provides a visual association for his motive, which would otherwise have only a textual basis.

Amfortas quotes the oracular prophecy of the coming of a 'pure fool' ('Durch Mitleid wissend, der reine Tor'), and as a quotation, audibly enclosed by inverted commas, the motive makes as much impression as a visible gesture.

The motives of Amfortas and the 'fool' have already been anticipated by Gurnemanz in the first part of his narration to the squires, before Amfortas is carried on, but that is not significant. Although they have accompanied explicit references in the text, their character at that first appearance was still half that of what, in *Opera and Drama*, Wagner called 'presentiments'. It goes to show that the exposition of a motive is not necessarily the first time it is heard, but only when it is represented on the stage in some way.

There are indeed some musical motives which are established, and their meaning expressed, only in words and not by anything visible when they are expounded. In the first act, when Gurnemanz is talking about the magic garden and the temptations to which Amfortas succumbed there, the Sorcery motive (whose harmonic basis recalls another expression of deception, the Tarnhelm motive from the *Ring*) and Klingsor's motive (the fourth bar of which reproduces the first bar of the Sorcery motive, with the third and fourth notes transposed down an octave: see next page) are not scenic but epic motives.

The important thing is not that there are exceptions to the rule of combined musical and scenic exposition but that they are exceptions and not the rule. For the exposition in *Parsifal* is 'really' nothing but a narration: on its own terms, strictly speaking, the narration has no need of supplementary illustration, but the presence of the tableaux is striking evidence of the nature of Wagner's musico-dramatic structural principles.

The character of tableau is in fact appropriate to a musical drama that grew into a 'festival drama of dedication'. In the letter of 30 May 1859 to Mathilde Wesendonk that has already been quoted, Wagner wrote first: 'Strictly speaking, Amfortas is the centre and the principal subject of the work.' Later, however, after an excursus on the shortcomings of Wolfram von Eschenbach's poem, which betrays the shortcomings of Wagner's appreciation of the generic principles of epic poetry, he went on:

> And there's one more difficulty about Parsifal. He is absolutely indispensable as Amfortas's longed-for redeemer, but if Amfortas is to be placed in the light he truly deserves he will become of such immense tragic interest that it will be almost impossible to stimulate an equal interest in another figure; and yet Parsifal must be made equally interesting, if his intervention is not simply to be like that of a *deus ex machina*, leaving everybody cold. And so Parsifal's development, his most sublime transfiguration – although predestined by every aspect of his thoughtful, deeply compassionate nature – must be restored to the foreground.

If Amfortas is a second Tristan, predestined to be the tragic hero *par excellence* of a music drama, the transfer of emphasis from Amfortas to Parsifal as the 'centre and principal subject of the work' means the transformation of music drama to 'festival drama of dedication'.

4

While the action of the festival drama of dedication is thus characterized by its inclination towards ritual and tableau, its language tends towards narrative and oracular adages. The scenes in the Grail Temple offer a verbal and stage ceremonial centring on the choruses, which are modelled, both verbally and musically, on liturgy. The last act culminates in a wonder-working utterance that marks the fulfilment of a prophecy: 'Die Wunde schließt der Speer nur, der sie schlug.' (Here, unlike the *Ring*, the oracle is not a snare but a sign of grace.) And though in one respect, as outbursts of suffering, Amfortas's complaints in the first and last acts form the most extreme contrast to the solemnity of the choruses, they do take their place within the framework of the ritual; the extremity of his suffering is occasioned by the ritual, recurring each time it is repeated and not an exceptional, unrepeatable occurrence. It is individual, personal to Amfortas, and at the same time it is representative.

There seems to be a connection between the epic, ritual character of the language and the replacement of alliterative verse by end-rhyme. (The Stabreim has not vanished altogether, as is sometimes claimed, but it is exceptional rather than the rule.) According to the theory Wagner developed in *Opera and Drama*, Stabreim is the verbal expression of emphasis and concentrated feeling, because each alliterative syllable carries an accent of meaning and the syllables necessarily follow each other closely. End-rhyme, on the other hand, has a formal, distancing effect.

However, the reversion to end-rhyme did not mean the restoration of regular periodic structures. On the contrary, the length of the lines is irregular and the number of accented syllables in them varies; there is a discernible tendency towards continual change, so that, as in the *Ring*, the external form of the language works against the evolution of schematic musical syntax, rather than assisting it. 'Quadratic' metre has dissolved into 'musical prose'. And thus the musical form owes its backbone not to the syntax but to the motivic associations that spread a densely woven net across the whole drama.

In greatly simplified terms, the use of musical motives in *Parsifal* is governed and conditioned by the contrast of chromaticism and diaton-icism: the chromaticism that conveys the deceptions of Klingsor's kingdom also expresses the anguish of Amfortas, while the expressive range of the diatonicism reaches from the naive simplicity of Parsifal's motive to the sublimity of the Grail themes. As categories of musical technique, chromaticism and diatonicism also have an allegorical sig-nificance: the very fact that two motives are both chromatic – an in-significant characteristic in itself, because it is so general – creates a dramatic association between them. The connection between deception and suffering, between the magic garden and Amfortas's lamentation, is as unmistakable as, in the diatonic sphere, that between the naivety of the 'pure fool' and the Grail kingship that awaits Parsifal at the end of his path to recognition. The fact that Wagner based the differentiations and ramifications of the dramatic argument, which have caused so much torment to the exegetes, on so simple, so obvious a contrast, which holds good for the stage action as well as for the music, is the proof of his theatrical genius.

But there is no question of simple extremes being put side by side without any form of mediation between them. During the years when he was writing *Parsifal*, as Cosima recorded, Wagner spoke more than once of his reluctance to have jarring effects, and of how he always tried to mediate them and make them comprehensible rather than leave the abruptness to make its own effect. If something was to be comprehensible, for Wagner, it had to be motivated and prepared for, to proceed as a natural consequence and fulfilment of something that had gone before, instead of erupting from nowhere. No less than *Tristan*, *Parsifal* is governed by Wagner's 'art of transition', which would not be the art that it is, however, if it did not have to overcome the difficulties presented by the extreme contrasts of character in the themes and motives.

The lament that bursts from Parsifal in the second act when Kundry's kiss has made him 'cosmically clear-sighted' divides formally into three periods. The first ('Amfortas!') and second ('Nein! Nein! Nicht die Wunde ist es') are governed and characterized by chromatic motives, those of lament and of sorcery, the third ('Es starrt die Blick') by quotations of Grail motives; yet the contrast is mediated, not abrupt. As in Amfortas's lament in the first act, the diatonic motives are drawn into the musically contrasting sphere of chromaticism: they are first heard chromatically distorted, darkened by the harmonies of Amfortas's motive or those of the motives associated with Klingsor and sorcery, then they are heard in minor-key variants, that is, in a modification that is weaker, less foreign. (When a motive or theme is transformed from tonic major to tonic minor the effect is of a chromatic darkening of the major, so that the quotation of the Grail Supper theme in the minor during Parsifal's lament belongs in the realm of chromaticism.)

5

Have I already told you that the fabulous, savage messenger of the Grail has to be one and the same creature as the seductress in the second act? Since that dawned upon me almost everything

to do with it has become clear to me. (Wagner to Mathilde
Wesendonk, early August 1860)

Kundry, the servant of the Grail, 'rose of hell' and penitent Magdalene,
is the most complex and contradictory figure in all Wagner's dramas,
a challenge to psychoanalytical interpretation. She is the Orgeluse of
Wolfram's epic, but also the Herodias of Christian legend, the temptress
of John the Baptist, and she is another Ahasuerus, who mocked the
sufferings of Christ and is condemned to wander eternally in search of
absolution. Kundry has her being a very long way away from the
traditional sphere of opera, the expression of simple passions; and it
was only after some hesitation that Wagner decided to undertake the
composition of *Parsifal*, as the letter to Mathilde Wesendonk betrays.
'This once I might prefer to leave it as a poem.'

Music, according to Schopenhauer, who was expressing the agreed
opinion of centuries, is an art which represents pure, unmixed feelings,
passions in the abstract, freed from the trammels of the reality to which
they owe their specific identity and motivation. Negation and dialectics,
ambiguity and paradox are alien to it, so long as the music is in isolation
and not associated with a text or stage action. It is understandable that
Wagner – who would have been appalled by Brecht's idea of using music
to contradict, denounce or protest against words or actions – shrank from
composing Kundry's scenes, the dominant characteristic of which is
sublime paradox, until he recognized that leitmotivic technique provided
him with the means to admit music to a realm which is otherwise closed
to it. Once leitmotive have been sufficiently clearly expounded they are
musical metaphors, and by their blending, mingling or allusion to each
other they make it possible to express divided feelings or ambiguities
which are otherwise beyond the scope of music.

When Parsifal repulses Kundry, the dialectic of the arguments with
which she tries to seduce him is so hard to unravel that it is hardly
conceivable how the music can participate in it, instead of merely
bypassing it in a wash of lyric phrases. Kundry desires absolution but
seeks it in Parsifal's arms, which is precisely what would bar her from
absolution; she recalls the curse that drives her, like Ahasuerus,
endlessly hoping to arouse a compassion that is a medium of temptation;
she longs for the forgiveness of Christ, at whose sufferings she laughed,
yet the image of reconciliation that she sees before her darkens and
distorts into a Black Mass.

Wagner's ability to express ambiguities which would seem to be beyond the power of music coincides with the ability to create form – that is, to create articulation and interrelationships – in 'endless melody', which seems, if heard superficially, to flow on in an amorphous stream. There is no separating the analysis of the form from that of the expressive or allegorical content. Kundry's response to Parsifal's refusal of her ('Grausamer') is divided into seven periods. The first four are 17 + 13 + 20 + 22 bars long. They are divided from each other by verbal and syntactical caesuras that coincide with caesuras in the musical form, as well as by the use of distinctive orchestral motives. On the other hand, they are linked by the use of one recurrent motive, that of Kundry herself, which brackets them together, providing the transitions from the first period to the second and from the second to the third, and appearing in the fourth as a subsidiary motive. Bracketing like this, however, is not the only means of linking periods together as parts of a larger musical form using the categories of rhetoric. If periods are on the one hand distinguished from each other by the variation of motives – specifically by the change of the principal motive in each – on the other hand the motives featured in the different periods are related to each other, without losing their distinctive qualities. The Yearning motive in the first period ('Bist du Erlöser'), which is the first phrase of *Tristan* with a modification of the harmony, is nothing other than an inversion of the Suffering motive in the second ('Des Heilands'). Formally this inversion means both derivation and contrast, association and distinction.

If the listener is able to hear the inversion as such, it is because he is waiting for a motivic association (in other words the composer relies on his possessing a sense of form, instead of allowing the current of the 'endless melody' to carry him along unthinking) and, vice versa, the motivic association – the formal link between the periods – is recognized because the inversion is audible. The formal association is also a means of clarifying, or drawing attention to, the expressive and allegorical content of the motives. The Suffering motive unites the suffering of Christ and that of Amfortas in a vertiginously paradoxical musical metaphor (the connection was made clear in Parsifal's lament after Kundry's kiss): as the inversion of it, the motive of Kundry's yearning becomes, by an analogous ambiguity, the expression of a longing for absolution which becomes inextricably involved in its own antithesis.

The principal motive in the third period is a hybrid, which carries out the formal function of mediating between the motives of suffering and yearning on the one hand, and the Grail Supper theme, the principal motive of the fourth period, on the other.

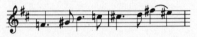

This motive ('durch Tod und Leben'), simultaneously expressing Kundry's frenzy, her longing for absolution and her predicament, represents the ultimate in the interlocking of heterogeneous elements; subjected to pedantic analysis, notes 1 to 5 emerge as a fragment of the Sorcery motive, notes 3 to 8 as a fragment of the galloping figure, and notes 3 to 6 as a fragment of the Yearning motive. Moreover, in the fourth period (after 'sein Blick') the Sorcery and Grail Supper motives blend into one another.

The harmony comes from the Sorcery motive, the rhythm from the Grail Supper motive; and the melody mediates between these two representatives of opposed musico-dramatic spheres.

In another letter to Mathilde Wesendonk, Wagner boasted of the 'art of transition' as the 'most subtle and most profound' of his skills; he could have claimed as much for the art of ambiguous expression and paradoxical intermingling that he discovered for music.

The works in the theatre

1

Of all Wagner's utterances, the most severely misunderstood must be the principal thesis of *Opera and Drama*. Presenting musical drama as the answer to the degeneracy that had befallen opera, he said that music was 'a medium of expression' and drama 'the purpose of expression'. In the effort to form a concept of the kind of drama of which music would be a function, people have been inclined to equate 'drama' with 'text' and have believed that the Wagnerian view of operatic history consists of establishing whether the text or the music is the dominant partner in a given work.

In Wagner's conception of musical drama, however, the text is just like the music, another 'medium of expression'. That makes the question as to whether the text is subordinate to the music or the music to the text secondary if not irrelevant; it is beside the point, which is that both text and music are functions of the drama. What in fact did Wagner mean by the drama to which he sought to subordinate all the other arts? Primarily it was the visible stage action, which he understood as the representation of undistorted 'human nature'. In his essay on Beethoven he wrote, in 1870:

> We know that the verses of poets, even those of a Goethe or a Schiller, cannot determine music; only drama may do that, and by drama I mean not the dramatic poem or text but the drama we see taking place before our eyes, the visible counterpart of the music, where the words and the text enunciated belong solely to the action and no longer to the poetic idea.

(By the 'poetic idea' Wagner meant the dramatist's 'intention', which ceases to be intention when its potential is realized in the visible action.) There is an obvious affinity here to the views of Verdi, the despised opposite extreme to Wagner; he set great store by the 'parola scenica', the kind of language which could best contribute to the action, and attached only secondary importance to its literary quality.

The central category in Wagner's aesthetic theory of musical drama is 'realization'. A Hegelian by upbringing, Wagner believed that what is interior has to externalize itself, to take on a form if it is not to be void. Whatever the poetic intention, the meaning locked away in the heart of a work, the important thing is the realization of that intention, the form in which it is presented to the perceptions of others. Wagner spoke of dance, the representation of mankind in its true, physical nature, as the 'most real' of all the arts. He regarded stage action as a 'form of dance imbued with ideals', so that movement and gesture on the stage can also come under the heading of the 'art of realization' – which for Wagner was the essence of art itself. Drama, as envisaged by Wagner, was fulfilled in stage action, with language and music also having the characteristics of gesture assigned to them. In his 1872 essay *On Actors and Singers* Wagner wrote:

> After giving this due consideration we have to recognize that it is the performers who play the essential artistic part in the theatre; the author's relationship to the essential 'art' is determined by the extent to which he has above all made use of the effect he expects the mimetic presentation to have on the finished form of his work.

Thus the combined text of the words and the music on paper does not amount to a self-sufficient, complete creation; only in production, in realization in a theatre, is musical drama completed and fulfilled. The history of the productions of a work is the continuing history of the work itself, in all its successive transformations.

2

The Bayreuth tradition, jealously guarded by first Cosima and then Siegfried Wagner, can be interpreted as an attempt to hold history at bay and prevent its power of transformation from having any effect on the 'festival dramas' and the 'festival drama of dedication'. Cosima

Wagner's implacable refusal to countenance any new ideas, such as those of Adolphe Appia, may look like sheer obstinacy, but it was not as unthinking or unjustified as it appears to a later generation with its conception of a theatre in permanent revolution. As long as the staging of a piece is seen as its mere shell, in accordance with the schematic idea of a body/soul relationship that dominated aesthetic theory in the nineteenth century, its production history is nothing but the description of a series of changing exterior forms in which the work has presented itself, without any effect on its identity and substance; the soul remains inviolate. But if the staging is regarded as part of the work itself, as its completion and fulfilment, then either one must accept the idea that works of art will be changed by history – an idea which it is hard to grasp, let alone embrace, since it contradicts the deeply rooted belief that one of the features rendering a work of art great is that it is above history – or one must surrender to a rigid traditionalism, which denies history or resists it, and attempts to preserve not only the work itself but also its production – both the principles and actual features of the production – from changes which would be changes to the essence of the work itself, and not merely to its exterior casing. The aesthetic maxim that tampering with the letter of a work of art will necessarily damage the spirit was extended in the Bayreuth tradition from the verbal and musical text to include the staging as well.

The Bayreuth style was well enough defined for its principles to be adopted as the basis of the instruction in a 'school of style'. The paradigm of the style was not so much the 1876 production of the *Ring*, which was obviously not a complete success, as that of *Parsifal* in 1882, Wagner's testament as a stage director. Cosima Wagner's influence began with the Bayreuth *Tristan* of 1886 and the *Meistersinger* of 1888, though the latter was based on Wagner's own Munich production of 1868. The Bayreuth style, as understood by Cosima, was characterized by slow tempos, distinct enunciation of the text, and a style of gesture that on the one hand tried to avoid the over-emphasis customary in the opera house but on the other hand was inclined to pedantry in its illustration of the musical motives; it represented the canonization of Wagner's precepts, and there is as much justice in the apologist's praise of its authenticity as in the polemicist's deploring of its dogmatism, the hardening of something specific and conditional into something general and unconditional.

It was the Bayreuth productions of *Tannhäuser* in 1891, *Lohengrin* in

1894 and *Der fliegende Holländer* in 1901 that fuelled the dogmatic dispute as to whether the earlier works were 'romantic operas' or 'music dramas'. The habits of audiences, who did not want their enjoyment of opera to be diminished, came into conflict with the Bayreuth thesis that Wagner's oeuvre, from *Der fliegende Holländer* onwards, had proceeded from a unifying conception, that of music drama.

The observation that the *Holländer*, *Tannhäuser* and *Lohengrin* are the products of a transitional stage in which romatic opera 'still' looms large and music drama is 'already' anticipated is hardly earth-shaking. But the Bayreuth thesis was not so inept, even if its premisses – the assertion of the unity of the oeuvre as a whole, and the denial of its inner evolutionary history – were shaky. There are good grounds for placing the operatic characteristics of the *Holländer*, which were already relics of tradition in 1841 when it was written, in a different light and incorporating them into a 'musico-dramatic' concept of production. The arias and the melodic style of the music given to Daland and Erik will then appear not as remnants of a convention, sops to cantilena-loving audiences, but as the expression of the banality distinguishing the prosaic 'exterior' world represented by Daland and Erik from the mythic 'interior' action, which takes place within Senta and the Dutchman and whose musical language is liberated from operatic diction. But to interpret the work as music drama – thus claiming to understand the work better than its composer did at the time when he wrote it – is implicitly to accept the idea of the transformation of works of art by history – the very idea against which Bayreuth traditionalism set its face.

3

The controversy aroused by the productions in which, from 1951 onwards, Wieland Wagner directly defied the Bayreuth tradition has almost died away; the outcome is unmistakable. No one can doubt Wieland Wagner's significance, but nor will anyone raise his pioneering rigorism to a dogma. There has been no lack of imitations, but they go halfway to repudiation. (Patrice Chéreau's centenary production of the *Ring* at Bayreuth, which drew attention to the drama of family relationships embedded in the mythic tragedy, and served to remind us that Wagner was the contemporary of Ibsen, created enormous indignation in 1976, yet by the following year this, too, had already begun to give way to a measure of acceptance.)

It is impossible to characterize Wieland Wagner's productions in a few sentences, because they were work in progress – it can be said that his starting points were a unique pictorial conception and a psychological interpretation in depth of the myths; but it is essential to say something about the fundamental charge that was made against him, the charge of ruthlessly ignoring things that are unambiguously stated in the scores.

It is simultaneously accurate and misplaced: accurate, because Wieland Wagner undeniably jettisoned the 'composed stage directions' as a dead past, which it would have been absurd to restore; misplaced, because stubborn fidelity to the production ideas that are contained in the music would have been traditionalism of a questionable kind.

The idea of the 'total artwork', the integration in musical drama of a particular theatrical style, which thus becomes a feature of the work and not merely of its performance, comes to grief over the failure to recognize that not all the arts have the character of works of art in a strict sense. Mimetic art – although Wagner 'composed' stage movement and gesture into his works – is not a work of art in itself, or even part of a work, to the extent that music or language can be. This means that it cannot outlive the age in which the work was written. The position is exemplified by the part played in the various arts by written notation. There has been no lack of attempts to record stage movements, notably dance choreography, but choreographic notation, unlike verbal or musical notation, is not a text that contains and preserves a work in itself; it consists of instructions on how to realize a choreography, while musical notation comprises both the text and the instructions on how to perform it in one. If stage presentation lacks identity as a work in its own right, the postulate of 'fidelity' has no footing; the gestures and stage movement Wagner 'composed' into his works are the petrified remains of a style of production that has since deceased. There is a lack of synchronism between the arts, not the stylistic lack of which Nietzsche complained, but in the sense that the different arts involved are at different stages of evolution towards self-sufficiency, towards a state where the practice of the arts in question can be formularized as a text.

Although the idea of a 'total artwork' embracing the physical staging of a work is thus shown to be aesthetically dubious, we may still ask whether the history of the dissemination and influence of Wagnerian music drama reveals a steady widening of the gap between the music as a work complete in itself and staging as a facet of performance practice (Wieland Wagner was accused of the discrepancy in terms suggesting that he was responsible for it), or whether the musical reception has itself been subject to historical changes, which have actually narrowed the gap between the music and the staging of the works.

In the first decades of its existence Wagner's music was heard primarily as an aggregation of leitmotive, appearing on cue like allegorical lantern slides: this is betrayed as much by Hans von Wolzogen's earnest listing of 'clues' as by the witticisms of Shaw and Debussy. Emphasis fell on the illustrative, commentating character of the motives, while their syntactic and formal role, their knotting together of a 'symphonic weave', was ignored. The total musical fabric was perceived vaguely as a flowing current, its details isolatedly, in relation to the words and stage action. But in recent years musical hearing has grown more abstract and now orients itself primarily by the example of instrumental music, not vocal music. (The process is revealed at its most extreme in the reception of programme music: it is now common to ignore the programme and listen to the music as 'absolute' music; but the programme was originally a component of the work itself and not simply an auxiliary commentary, so if a piece can survive this treatment it is no bad test of its formal musical quality.) To exactly the same degree that listening to music has become a matter of listening for its forms, the staging of a musical drama can ignore 'composed stage directions' without destroying the sense of the music, when that sense consists of relationships: firstly of the relation between the music and the stage action, and secondly of the formal structures of the music itself. The trend towards abstraction characteristic of the productions of Wieland Wagner can also be observed in the course followed by the reception of the music.